Patsy Westcott is on
magazine's top

By the same author

Pregnancy and Birth
Your Baby's First Year
Feeding Your Baby and Child

The
Mother & Baby
Book of

YOUR CHILD'S
HEALTH

An A–Z Guide

Patsy Westcott

GRAFTON BOOKS

A Division of the Collins Publishing Group

LONDON GLASGOW
TORONTO SYDNEY AUCKLAND

Grafton Books
A Division of the Collins Publishing Group
8 Grafton Street, London W1X 3LA

A Grafton Paperback Original 1990

A CIP catalogue record for this book is available from the British Library

ISBN 0-586-20663-9

Printed and bound in Great Britain by
Collins, Glasgow

Set in Goudy Old Style

CONTENTS

INTRODUCTION

As a parent you are in a unique position to influence your child's health – not only during childhood, but for the rest of her life. Your child's individual health profile is built in part on the genetic characteristics she has inherited from you and her father, and also on the lifestyle she adopts. Healthy habits laid down in childhood will set your child on the pathway to good health for the future.

However healthy your lifestyle, your child will nevertheless fall ill from time to time, and is bound to have the occasional accident. Such events are part and parcel of childhood, and it is to help you deal with them that this book has been written.

We at *Mother & Baby* magazine are aware that what mothers need most when a child becomes sick is clear, concise information that will tell them at a glance what course of action to adopt. And that is what this book, written with the help of *Mother & Baby*'s two medical experts, Dr Alexander Gunn and health visitor Jenny Jeffs, sets out to do.

As a parent you are the lynchpin of the health team, which also includes your doctor and health visitor. Most of your child's illnesses will be minor ones that can be dealt with at home using a modicum of common sense. The first part of the book therefore is a guide to looking after your child when she is ill. It covers what you can expect from your child, and has plenty of practical tips on caring for her and keeping her amused.

Good communication with your doctor is essential, so this section also tells you how to recognize those occasions when a doctor's visit is necessary, and what to tell the doctor. It gives information on what you should keep in a home medicine cabinet, and includes hints to help the medicine go down.

An increasing number of people are taking an interest in alternative therapies, especially for those illnesses that aren't always adequately treated by conventional medicine. Therefore Part I also includes a brief introduction to some of the most popular alternative therapies.

Finally there is a reminder of first-aid techniques and hints on dealing with minor accidents and injuries.

The second part of the book is an A–Z of childhood illnesses. It does not attempt to be fully comprehensive, but it aims to include all the common ailments you are likely to encounter in your child's first three years of life. It does not cover major disabilities such as autism and spina bifida, since these involve major treatment and care of the kind that this ready-reference format cannot do justice to.

Your intimate relationship with your child puts you in the best possible position to know when she is ill, and most doctors have learnt to trust mothers' instincts. The main aim of this book is to give you the information you need to back up those instincts, and enable your child to have a happy, healthy childhood.

Patsy Westcott, 1990.

Note: In order to reflect the experiences of all mothers, 'he' and 'she' have been used alternately in this book to refer to the child.

Part I

CARING FOR YOUR SICK CHILD

WHAT TO DO WHEN YOUR CHILD IS ILL

Illness is a normal part of everyday life, and many illnesses cure themselves given time. Children tend to be more prone to minor illnesses than adults because they have not built up any natural immunity. Becoming ill helps your child's body build up these defences. A calm, matter-of-fact attitude towards illness will help you take things in your stride and help your child to recover quickly. You do not need any special nursing skills to look after a sick child – just common sense and a little knowledge. This book will help give you some of the latter, and with practice you will learn to make your child comfortable when he is ill.

Babies are born with a certain degree of natural immunity from you. Breast milk contains antibodies that boost this natural resistance, but sooner or later your baby will encounter a bug he has not met before and become poorly. When he is ill he needs two things from you – your attention . . . and lots of extra love. It will help if you streamline your life and cut out unnecessary chores so you can give him the time and care he needs to regain his energy.

Whatever age your child is, expect him to become more babyish when he is ill and treat him accordingly. A toddler may behave like a crawler. A baby who is on solids may want to go back to drinking from breast or bottle. And a younger baby may want to be held and carried all the time. Make allowances for these changes in behaviour. Your child will be his usual self once he is better.

On the practical front you need to keep your child's room at a steady temperature and well-ventilated. If your child has a high temperature he will be more comfortable in loose pyjamas or a nightie made from cotton or a cotton mix to enable his skin to 'breathe' and sweat easily. A baby may feel more comfortable in a vest and nappy. If your child is feverish replace his duvet or sheets and blankets with a single cotton sheet.

Your child will probably be off his food if he is ill. Don't worry if he doesn't eat much – he will regain his appetite as he gets better – but he does need plenty to drink. A baby will probably take in more fluids if he is offered frequent drinks from breast or bottle. A toddler may be tempted if you put his drink in a special cup or give him a curly straw to suck through. Small drinks from an egg cup or a small glass may be more tempting than a beaker of juice, which may become warm and stale. Make up fruit ice cubes or ice lollies.

Should your child stay in bed when he is ill? A really poorly child will probably not feel like being up and may be happy to stay in bed, but he may become lonely. To avoid this, and to prevent you having to run up and down stairs all the time, make up a bed downstairs so he can see and hear you. You could bring his bedding down and arrange it on the sofa. Alternatively make up a camp bed in a corner of the sitting room. At night you may get more sleep if you move to a makeshift bed in your child's room, or even allow him to sleep in your bed for the time being. Change his bedding frequently, as it will get stuffy and sweaty. Put a towel and waterproof sheet under his bottom sheet if he is out of nappies, as he may occasionally wet the bed. Needless to say, don't scold him if this happens. He is not being deliberately naughty, but his illness is making him return to more babyish ways.

How illness occurs

Illnesses occur as a result of the body being invaded by:

- *Bacteria* e.g. whooping cough, tetanus, septic throat, scarlet fever
- *Viruses* e.g. colds, chicken pox, flu
- *Fungi* e.g. athlete's foot, ringworm, thrush
- *Parasites* e.g. threadworms, lice

How infection spreads

Infection spreads from person to person via several routes:

- *Air* droplets containing germs, which get into the air as a result of sneezing, coughing and breathing, and are breathed in by others. Chicken pox, measles and colds are examples of infections spread in this way.
- *Food or water* that has been contaminated through poor hygiene, undercooking, lack of sanitation, or contamination during processing or packing.
- *Infected soil or dust* which enters the mouth, a cut or a graze, e.g. tetanus.
- *Through the skin* – either through breaks in the skin where there is a cut, graze or other wound, or through animal or insect bites e.g. mosquitos, which spread malaria and yellow fever in tropical countries.
- *From mother to baby during pregnancy via the placenta* e.g. German measles, AIDS, *or during birth* when the baby may pick up the infection while passing down the birth canal, e.g. herpes.

Tips on looking after your sick child

- Remember drinking is more important than eating.
- To tempt your child to eat, make his food look more interesting. Make miniature sandwiches, or give him an open sandwich decorated to look like a face. Jelly, ice-cream and other non-rich party fare also go down well.
- Provide a 'treasure' bag of special toys. Remember he will want to play with toys that are suitable for a younger child.
- A cassette player, TV or video will help keep him occupied for short periods, so you can have a break. But they are no substitute for your attention.
- Your child will not be able to concentrate for long, so vary his activities. It may help to jot down a list of games and toys so you don't run out of ideas.
- If your child's illness looks likely to last for more than a day or so, keep in touch with friends so you don't feel isolated. You may even be able to arrange for someone to come and babysit for a short while to enable you to go out.
- Once your child is feeling better, and is no longer infectious, invite a friend round to play with him. Keep the visit short.
- Follow your doctor's advice on how long to keep your child away from other children. Generally speaking, there is no need to isolate a poorly child from other members of the family, as they will have been exposed to him while he was incubating the illness anyway.
- If your child catches German measles keep him away from women in the first three months of pregnancy.
- Make allowances for your child's more babyish behaviour.

At the height of his illness probably all your child will want to do is sleep. However, as he recovers he will want to be entertained. Bear in mind that he should not be overstretched, and provide him with games and toys that are suitable for a slightly younger child. Keep back a few of his old toys for this purpose. Many mothers keep a special 'treasure' pack of games and trinkets that are brought out only when their child is ill. You can put in it books and toys, perhaps left over from Christmas or a birthday, and collect any bits and pieces that catch your eye when you are out shopping.

As your child begins to feel a little better there is no reason why he should not get outside, so long as the weather is fine. A sick child, especially one with a chest infection, should not go out if it is foggy or cold.

Keeping your child amused

The following toys and games are especially suitable for a sick baby or toddler.

- Mobile
- Sparkly jewellery or Christmas decorations hung where they catch the light
- Bottles of coloured water (use food colouring) placed in a window
- A goldfish in a bowl or aquarium
- Large beads to thread on to a string
- A puzzle to fiddle with
- Magnetic shapes, jigsaws or games, particularly the sort you can buy to play with in the car
- A selection of tiny cars on a tray
- Playdough – make up your own (see below), or buy it ready made
- Magic painting books – which you paint using just plain water
- Magazines and catalogues – to cut out pictures and stick them in a scrap book
- A photo album to look at – even a baby as young as one year old will enjoy looking at photos of himself and his family
- A special toy that you keep especially for when your child is ill, such as a soft toy, doll or puppet. This can also be useful with a toddler to act as a 'go-between' if he will not talk to you about his illness

Recipe for Playdough
2 cups plain flour
1 cup salt
2 teaspoons cream of tartar
2 tablespoons cooking oil
2 cups water mixed with food colour of your choice
Place the dry ingredients in a saucepan and stir in the remaining ingredients. Stir continuously over a medium heat until the mixture thickens and starts to peel away from the side of the pan. Remove the pan from the heat, turn the dough out on to a board, and knead until it is a pliable consistency. Store in the refrigerator in a polythene bag. This keeps for weeks.

WHEN SHOULD YOU CALL THE DOCTOR?

There are times when your baby or toddler is so obviously unwell that there is no doubt you should call the doctor. But what about those other occasions when the situation is not so clear cut? The bank holiday weekend when he seems unusually fretful and somehow not quite himself? The Saturday night when he starts to run a temperature? Is it really necessary to call the doctor out, or will you be branded a fussy, over-anxious mother?

No good family doctor ever minds being called out to a sick baby, even if it does turn out to be a false alarm. Doctors have learnt to take account of a mother's intuition. Often you will be the first to notice that your baby or child is unwell, even before any obvious symptoms appear, so don't be afraid to trust your instincts and contact the doctor. If it is a weekday, and your child's condition does not appear urgent, make an appointment for the next surgery. The receptionist should fit you in that day if you explain that the appointment is for a baby or small child. Out of surgery hours you can phone the doctor for advice and guidance and describe your child's symptoms on the phone.

The following are situations when you would be justified in calling the doctor.

- A temperature over 39°C (102.2°F)
- A temperature of 38°C (100.4°F) if accompanied by a stiff neck or a headache, or if your child cannot drink
- A convulsion
- If your child loses consciousness and cannot be aroused
- A temperature of less than 35°C (95°F), or if your child seems cold and drowsy
- Any marked fluctuation in temperature
- A temperature of over 38°C (100.4°F) that lasts for more than three days
- Diarrhoea and vomiting continuing for more than a day or night. Diarrhoea and vomiting are always serious symptoms in a baby, so don't delay in calling the doctor. There is a real danger of dehydration if you don't get medical help
- Diarrhoea and vomiting accompanied by pain in the abdomen or a raised temperature
- Loss of appetite in a baby under six months old
- Sickness, dizziness and headache
- Griping pains in the abdomen
- If your baby or child's breathing becomes laboured, or if his skin turns blue and his ribs are drawn in as he breathes
- If you are worried for any reason, even though you cannot quite put your finger on what is wrong
- If there is blood in your child's urine, vomit or bowel movements

WHAT THE DOCTOR WILL NEED TO KNOW

If you are feeling anxious it is easy to forget things, so it may help to jot down all the relevant details and anything you want to ask the doctor. The doctor will need to know your child's age (and his sex and weight if you are consulting him or her by phone). Give the doctor a brief rundown of your child's symptoms, such as swollen glands, vomiting, diarrhoea or pain. He or she will also need to know any other facts that may throw some light on the symptoms, such as if your child has had a fall, been stung by an insect or bitten and so on. Tell the doctor what treatment, if any, you have given your child, such as any steps you may have taken to bring his temperature down. Also tell the doctor if your child is taking any medicine, or has to have any medication for a chronic condition, and inform him or her of any previous reactions your child may have had to drugs or treatment, for instance if he is allergic to certain types of antibiotic.

AT THE DOCTOR'S

Your doctor may agree to make a home visit. However, if he or she asks you to take your child to the surgery bear in mind that there will be better facilities there to examine your child and carry out any tests that could help in diagnosis. If the doctor wants to see your child at the surgery, you may be able to arrange with the receptionist to go straight in to see him or her, or to wait with your child in a separate room so that he is not exposed to any other germs in the waiting room.

The doctor will need to examine your child and, if he is old enough to talk, to ask him questions about the illness. You can help interpret what the doctor says to your child, but do allow your child the opportunity to put into words or to indicate how he is feeling to the doctor himself. The doctor will be able to observe your child's behaviour, both verbal and non-verbal, which will aid diagnosis. He or she should then be able to give you some indication of what is wrong, or else may suggest further tests.

Listen carefully to what the doctor has to say, and ask him or her to repeat any instructions or explanations you don't understand. Don't be afraid to do this. When you are feeling worried you may forget things, so do note down any special information so you can refer to it later.

If the doctor prescribes any medication he or she should tell you what it is for, what effect it will have, and how long it will be before it starts to work. If your doctor does not volunteer this information, don't be afraid to ask. Do not expect a prescription automatically every time you visit the doctor. The great majority of minor illnesses will cure themselves in time, and medicines that suppress the symptoms sometimes cause more problems than they solve. It is important to stress to your child too that his body has the capacity to heal itself given the opportunity, so as not to inculcate an attitude of too much dependence on the doctor.

Ask the doctor what course the illness can be expected to take and if there are any signs you should watch out for. Your doctor should tell you how long it will take for your child to recover, whether you should call him or her again, should the illness not improve, or get worse, and how to care for your child at home. Finally your doctor will tell you whether or not you need to make a follow-up visit to the surgery.

Your child and the doctor

Your child needs to see the doctor as a friend who is there to help him recover when he is unwell. But try to avoid presenting the doctor as a miracle worker with a pill for every ill. It will help your child come to terms with visiting the doctor if you play games with him. A teddy or a doll can be taken to the doctor and bandaged, or given an injection or some pretend medicine. There are also a number of simple books available for children dealing with everyday events like visiting the doctor's surgery.

HELPING THE MEDICINE GO DOWN

- If any medicine is prescribed make sure you know what it is for, how it works and how long before it starts to take effect.
- If your child experiences any side effects report them to the doctor.
- Make sure you understand the exact instructions for taking the medicine, and follow them to the letter.
- If a medicine is prescribed 'every four hours', check what this means. Will you have to wake your child up at night to give him his medicine?
- Ask your doctor if there are any foods your child should avoid while he is taking medicine, or any other special precautions you should take.
- Find out if your child needs to finish the entire course of medication

(this usually applies to antibiotics) or if he can stop taking it when he feels better (e.g. decongestants).

- Don't mix liquid medicine with drinks, as your child may not drink the full quota.
- Always measure out medicine exactly – no more and no less than the instructions state.
- If the medicine tastes really unpleasant you may be able to disguise the taste by mixing it with a small amount of something strong-tasting such as apple purée, chocolate dessert or ice-cream.
- It may help to make a note of the times and doses of medicine taken, especially if your child has to take several different ones.
- Always make sure your doctor knows about any other medicine your child is taking, to avoid reactions caused by mixing two incompatible ones.
- Report to the doctor if the medicine is not working.
- Store all medicines carefully, according to instructions. For instance some antibiotics need to be kept in the refrigerator.
- Pills or tablets can be finely crushed between two spoons and mixed with a little jam, chocolate spread or honey to disguise the taste.
- Don't crush capsules. If necessary, smear a little water, fruit juice or margarine on to the capsule shell to moisten it and help it slip down more easily.
- Special hollow or calibrated spoons are available to help avoid spills and make the medicine easier to administer.
- Always destroy any unused medicines or tablets, or return them to the chemist.
- If your child is reluctant to take the medicine, be gentle but firm. If he is old enough to understand you can stress how important it is to help him get better. The promise of a reward, such as a sweet, a game, or looking at a book together, may help.
- Give your child a drink of his favourite juice to help take away any bitter or unpleasant taste.

GIVING MEDICINE TO A BABY

Use a spoon, dropper or special holder. You may need help if your baby is wriggling around. Wrap him firmly in a shawl, or get someone to hold him while you give him the medicine. Don't lie your baby flat on his back, instead cradle him as you would if you were giving the bottle or breast. Put the spoon or holder into his mouth and let the medicine dribble down. If he spits it out, put the spoon further back in his mouth, then take out the spoon, close his mouth by putting your finger under his chin, and press to force him to swallow. If you are using a dropper, gently drip the medicine into his mouth. Alternatively you could dip your finger into the medicine and let him suck it off. Give him a drink from breast or bottle afterwards to take away any nasty taste.

DOES MY CHILD HAVE A TEMPERATURE?

Some children run a high temperature very quickly when they are ill. Others can be quite ill and yet still not feel unduly hot. Temperature is not necessarily an indication of the seriousness of the illness, and a high temperature is not an illness in itself. In fact it's a sign that the body is fighting back against the illness or infection.

Normal body temperature lies between 36–37.5°C (96.8–99.5°F). It fluctuates according to activity, emotion, food and the time of day, being lowest in the morning and highest around midnight.

You can estimate if your child is feverish by feeling his forehead with your hand. If it feels hotter than usual, and especially if he looks flushed, seems sleepy, or has other symptoms such as shivering, sweating, glassy eyes, or rapid breathing, you can be fairly certain he is running a temperature. With some illnesses evidence of a high temperature is enough. With others, you may need to make a more precise assessment; details about the degree and nature of your child's temperature (for example if it is fluctuating) can help your doctor diagnose your child's illness. Remember that an unduly low temperature can also be a warning sign.

There are various kinds of thermometer available with which to take your child's temperature. Probably the simplest to use is the heat strip, which you press against your child's forehead and which either changes colour or gives a reading. This is safe and easy to use, but it is not accurate enough if you need to know exactly what your child's temperature is.

The traditional mercury thermometer is extremely accurate. However, it can be dangerous and you should never put one in a baby or toddler's mouth in case he crunches on it and breaks the glass.

A digital thermometer is a worthwhile investment and is safe, accurate and easy to use. It costs a little more than the other two types, but it will give you many years of use.

HOW TO TAKE YOUR CHILD'S TEMPERATURE

Place the thermometer:

- Under his arm or groin – in this case his temperature will register a little lower than a mouth temperature.
- In his mouth for three minutes or, in the case of a digital thermometer, until it bleeps. *Never* use a mercury thermometer in a baby or small toddler's mouth. Don't take your child's temperature immediately after giving him a hot drink. If he has been breathing through his mouth this will also alter the reading.

HOW TO BRING DOWN YOUR CHILD'S TEMPERATURE

Dress your child in cool cotton clothing, or strip him down to vest and pants or nappy. Keep him covered in a thin cotton sheet and make sure the room is cool. Give your child plenty of fluids to drink. If your doctor advises it, give him paracetamol syrup, but make sure you do not exceed the stated dose, and don't give it more frequently than advised on the label. (Never dose a baby younger than three months with paracetamol syrup without first consulting your doctor.) When the time comes to give him the next dose, take his temperature first and make a note of it to enable you to plot the course of his fever. This is important information for your doctor.

If these simple measures do not succeed in reducing your child's temperature, or if his temperature is over 39°C (102.2°F), sponge him with tepid water. Don't be tempted to use cold water, as this could cause him to have a rebound high temperature. If your child continues to run a temperature after a couple of days, contact your doctor.

To sponge down your child

1. Protect whatever he is lying on with towels.
2. Undress him.
3. Using tepid (not cold) water, gently sponge him down, using a

flannel or sponge that is soaked but not dripping. As soon as the
flannel or sponge starts to get hot dip it in the water.

4. Take your child's temperature every five minutes, and stop the
sponging as soon as it drops to 38°C (100.4°F).

5. Don't dry your child – the water on the surface of his skin works like
sweat to cause cooling.

6. Cover him lightly with a sheet afterwards, but don't let him get
cold.

7. Repeat the procedure if his temperature rises.

8. If sponging doesn't cause his temperature to drop, consult the doctor
straight away.

MEDICAL SUPPLIES

For unexpected emergencies keep a simple first-aid kit in your house in
a convenient place out of the reach of children. Make sure all adults
who are likely to use it know where it is kept, and replace items as you
use them. Store items in a large empty tin (an old biscuit tin is ideal) or
carton. Alternatively you can buy ready-packed first-aid kits from larger
chemists.

Suggested first-aid kit

- Selection of plasters in various shapes and sizes
- Sterile dressings in assorted sizes
- Sterile gauze pads in various sizes
- Roll of gauze bandages in several widths
- Two or three elastic bandages
- Triangular bandage for use as a sling
- Crêpe bandage
- Cotton wool
- Safety pins
- Sharp needle
- Blunt-ended scissors
- Surgical tape
- Pair of tweezers
- Antiseptic wipes
- Thermometers – one digital and one plastic heat strip

Additional supplies

You will also need a stock of basic medical supplies, which will vary
according to the needs of your family.

Some or all of the following would prove useful:

- Calamine lotion
- High-factor sunscreen cream or lotion
- After-sun soothing cream
- Insect repellent and sting relief preparations
- Paracetamol syrup
- Paracetamol tablets
- Travel sickness pills
- Nappy rash cream
- Bottle of mild disinfectant
- Any special medications or equipment, e.g. inhalers, needed by any member of the family

In the car

Keep a similar first-aid kit in the car. In addition the following items would be useful:

- Torch and spare batteries
- Soap
- Towel
- Blanket
- Safety triangle
- Pen and paper

Safety tips

- Keep medicines out of the reach of children.
- Don't use medicines prescribed for anyone else.
- Always follow the instructions on the packet unless otherwise instructed by your doctor.
- Flush any unused medicines down the lavatory.
- Discard over-the-counter medicines once they reach their expiry date.

ALTERNATIVE HEALTHCARE

Many more people are now seeking out alternative (sometimes called complementary) therapies, following the realization that orthodox medicine does not have all the answers to treating some of the illnesses that are rife today, such as allergies. Alternative therapies are reputed to work in a slow, gentle way and this makes them especially suitable for many children's ailments. Many GPs nowadays are taking an interest in alternative medicine or will be happy to refer you to a reliable alternative practitioner if they cannot offer treatment themselves.

Alternative medicine differs from orthodox treatment in that it looks at the whole person rather than just treating the outward symptoms of disease. Though the individual therapies differ, there are two underlying beliefs that are common to most of them:

1. Illness occurs because of some sort of imbalance in the body.
2. Given time and support the body will heal itself.

These ideas are not new, and many orthodox doctors would also agree with them.

It is probably best to think of alternative forms of treatment as complementing orthodox therapy. There are times when orthodox treatment would be the best therapy for a particular condition, such as appendicitis, but there are other times when a more natural approach may be equally successful.

Common childhood ailments such as coughs, colds and virus infections, as well as many childhood illnesses such as chicken pox, measles, German measles and so on, seem to respond well to alternative treatment. Many chronic (recurrent) illnesses such as allergies have been successfully treated by alternative methods.

One thing most alternative therapies have in common is an emphasis on a good diet containing plenty of fresh fruit and vegetables, wholemeal cereals, and a small amount of lean meat and fish.

CONSULTING AN ALTERNATIVE PRACTITIONER

Because alternative therapies are 'holistic' – i.e. concerned with the whole person and not just with the symptoms of the illness – a consultation with an alternative practitioner is somewhat different from the average ten minutes in the doctor's surgery. An alternative practitioner will spend a long time finding out about your child – her lifestyle, diet, sleeping patterns, personality, family background etc – in the belief that all these factors have a bearing on her overall health and well being. You can expect to spend an hour or more for a first consultation with an alternative therapist. Of course you will be expected to pay for this service.

CHOOSING AN ALTERNATIVE PRACTITIONER

Many alternative practitioners have undergone a lengthy professional training in their particular therapy. However, because alternative therapists are not controlled by any central governing body anyone can set up as an alternative practitioner, and so it is best to go only to a practitioner who belongs to an alternative therapy association.

There is no foolproof way to find an alternative practitioner but the following tips may help:

- Ask your doctor to recommend one. Many GPs themselves practise some alternative therapies. Others are often interested and may be able to suggest a reliable practitioner in your area.
- Choose a practitioner who is registered with the relevant professional organizations (see below). This is your safeguard that the therapist has undergone training.
- Ask the practitioner you have chosen whether he or she has treated this particular illness before. The practitioner may be willing for you to contact other patients to find out how satisfied they were.
- Don't expect miracles or an instant cure. Most alternative therapies act slowly and gently.

- If your child is suffering from a particular complaint, such as food allergy, contact the relevant self-help organization, which may be able to suggest a reliable practitioner.

HOMOEOPATHY

Homoeopathy works on the principle that like cures like. The remedies, of which there are over 2,000, are given in microscopic doses. They are made from natural substances such as plants, flowers, minerals and salts. The theory is that, in an effort to stimulate the body's curative powers, the homoeopath administers a remedy that in a healthy person would produce the symptoms of the illness being treated. This is similar to the way in which vaccines stimulate the body to produce antibodies. However, unlike vaccines the remedies are prepared in minute doses which are shaken (or succussed) to make them potent, according to the methods laid down by the founder of homoeopathy, the eighteenth-century physician Samuel Hahnemann.

Homoeopathic medicines are safe and easy to take, especially for babies and children.

If you take your child to a homoeopath be prepared for a lengthy consultation. The homoeopath will want to build up a complete picture of your child, and will note down her behaviour and mental and emotional state as well as her physical symptoms. The remedy the homoeopath prescribes will be tailored to your child as an individual rather than to the illness itself, so different remedies may be prescribed for the same ailment depending on how your child is affected. Homoeopathy has been found to be particularly effective in treating common childhood conditions such as colic, croup, allergies, infectious diseases, abdominal upsets, constipation, diarrhoea, skin complaints and asthma.

SELF-HELP

Many health-food stores and chemists now carry a wide range of homoeopathic remedies for treating minor ailments at home. Select the one that most closely matches your child's symptoms. If that doesn't work, try something else or consult a homoeopath. It is also possible to buy homoeopathic first-aid kits for minor accidents. Always read labels with great care for dosage and suitability for child's use. Remedies come in the form of slightly sweet tablets, pills or granules. There are also creams, ointments and tinctures for external use.

- Store homoeopathic remedies away from direct light and strong-smelling products such as toothpaste, perfume, disinfectants.
- Allow half an hour after your child has eaten or cleaned her teeth before administering a medicine – they should be taken in a 'clean' mouth.
- Don't handle tablets. If any are spilled don't use them.
- Your child should chew the tablet or dissolve it under her tongue. Don't wash it down with squash or a flavoured drink as this could interfere with the remedy.

SOME HOMOEOPATHIC REMEDIES FOR BABIES AND CHILDREN

Colic

Three-month colic. Whining, wind, vomiting, rejects milk. Pitiful crying, stops when picked up.	Pulsatilla
Swollen tummy. Wind passed in small quantities brings no relief. Better for warmth. Not soothed by being picked up. Irritable and in obvious pain.	Chamomilla
Chilly, irritable, angry. Too much milk.	Nux vomica
Writhing and twisting. Cannot keep still. Improves on passing wind.	Colocynthis

If symptoms are severe and homoeopathic remedies bring no relief, or if baby has diarrhoea and vomiting for more than six hours, or blood or mucus in the stools, or is running any fever, contact your GP.

Nappy rash

Hot baby. Red skin worse in heat.   Sulphur
Worse after bathing. Better in
fresh air.

Any type of nappy rash.   Calendula or chamomile
                                             cream for external
                                             application.

Teething

Painful, cross, irritable. Cannot   Chamomilla
be settled. Helped by carrying.

Weepy and whiny. Stops when   Pulsatilla
cuddled. Wants affection.

Constipation

Strains for soft, sticky stool.   Alumina
Unable to pass stool until large.

Frequent desire to pass stool   Nux vomica
produces only small quantities.
Alternates with diarrhoea.

Croup If there is no easing or if the croup gets worse, call the doctor.

To allay anxiety.   Aconite

Loose rattling cough. Worse for   Hepar Sulph.
cold and draughts.

Dry, barking cough. Child wakes   Spongia
from sleep with violent cough.

For further information contact the British Homoeopathic Association,
27a Devonshire Street, London W1N 1RJ.

ACUPUNCTURE

Acupuncture, or needle insertion, has been part of traditional Chinese medicine for thousands of years. Today it is also attracting serious scientific attention in the West. It is based on the idea that there is a flow of energy around the body. If this energy becomes unbalanced, illness results. Acupuncture sets out to rebalance the energy flow by stimulating acupuncture points set along channels called meridians, which link the energy circuits.

The acupuncturist will spend a lot of time asking you about your child, and may include questions that seem strange, such as does a hot bath help? He or she will then examine your child and feel her pulses in order to detect which meridians are out of balance. The acupuncturist will then insert fine needles at various points, according to the diagnosis. Your child will feel a tiny prick. The needles are left in from a few seconds to several minutes. Your child may need several treatment sessions, depending on the severity of her illness. It is normal for your child to experience a slight worsening of symptoms after the first treatment, this is said to be a sign that the body is responding to treatment.

Acupuncture has also been widely used for pain control because of its effect on the nervous system.

Acupuncture has successfully been used to treat a number of childhood problems, including wheezy bronchitis, asthma, hay fever, eczema and many others.

For further information contact the Council for Acupuncture, Suite 1, 19a Cavendish Square, London W1M 9AD.

HERBAL MEDICINE

This is the oldest form of medicine, and many modern drugs have their origins in plants and herbs. Herbal treatments use the whole plant rather than extracting just one active ingredient as some orthodox drugs do. The treatments are gentle and safe, which makes them especially suitable for children. Herbal practitioners are generally well trained and experienced. Like all types of alternative practitioners a herbalist looks for the root cause of an illness rather than seeking simply to alleviate the symptoms.

For any but the most minor ailments it is better to consult a qualified herbalist.

Herbal medicines are prepared by making infusions (from herbs steeped in boiling water), decoctions (from herbs simmered in water), crushing herbs into tablets and capsules, or making them into poultices, ointments or lotions for external use.

Babies and children need only small doses of herbs, calculated according to their age and size.

SOME HERBAL REMEDIES FOR CHILDREN

Unless you are familiar with herbal remedies, always consult a practitioner before making these up.

Colds and coughs	Infusions of lemon balm, catnip, chamomile, elderflower, peppermint.
Colic	Infusions of fennel seeds, caraway, dill, catmint or chamomile.
Cuts and grazes	Calendula or comfrey ointment.
Nappy rash	Comfrey, calendula or marshmallow ointment.
Sore throat	Blackcurrant tea. Hot sage or thyme tea.
Teething	Calendula lotion rubbed on the gums. Chamomile or lemon balm tea to help sleep.
Bruises and sprains	Witch hazel.

For further information contact the National Institute of Medical Herbalists, 41 Hatherley, Road, Winchester, Hants SO22 6RR.

CLINICAL ECOLOGY (ENVIRONMENTAL MEDICINE)

This is one of the fastest-growing therapies and many of its practitioners are qualified orthodox doctors. Clinical ecology has developed in response to the dramatic increase in allergic conditions. It is thought that the widespread use of chemicals in food and the environment is responsible for this increase in apparent allergies, such as eczema, asthma, migraine, and many other vague aches and pains, as well as conditions such as hyperactivity. Treatment consists of testing which foods and substances the child is allergic to, either by removing them from the diet and then reintroducing them to see if they cause a reaction, or by performing skin tests or putting weak solutions of particular foods under the tongue then checking for a reaction. Offending substances are then cut out of the diet, or the child is put on a rotation diet in which foods that provoke upsets are eaten in strict rotation over a couple of weeks. Clinical ecologists may also offer desensitizing treatment, which involves giving a weak solution of allergy-provoking foods as drops under the tongue until the symptoms disappear.

Ask your doctor to refer you to a specialist or contact the Council for Complementary and Alternative Medicine, Suite 1, 19a Cavendish Square, London W1M 9AD.

OSTEOPATHY

Osteopaths believe that structural problems such as misalignment of the bones in the spine, muscle spasms, and so on can affect nerve function and blood flow to the vital organs, so causing disease. Osteopathy has been widely used as a treatment for back pain in particular.

Treatment consists of a full examination followed by manipulation of the joints and muscles to return them to normal.

Cranial osteopathy is a technique that involves gentle pressure on the patient's head in order to correct the ebb and flow of cerebrospinal fluid around the brain and spinal cord, which can lead to problems such as head pain, earache and so on. It is a very gentle type of osteopathy which is especially suitable for children and babies who may have suffered a traumatic birth.

For further information contact the British College and Association of Naturopathy and Osteopathy, 6 Netherhall Gardens, London NW3.

FURTHER INFORMATION ON

ALTERNATIVE MEDICINE

Institute for Complementary Medicine, 21 Portland Place, London W1N 3AF. Tel: 01-636 9543.
British Holistic Medical Association, 179 Gloucester Place, London NW1 6DX. Tel: 01-262 5299.
The Natural Family Doctor, ed. Dr Andrew Stanway, Century.
Everyday Homoeopathy, Dr David Gemmell, Beaconsfield Publishers.
The Home Herbal, A Handbook of Simple Remedies, Barbara Griggs, Pan.
Alternative Healthcare for Children, Eveline de Jong, Thorsons.
Help Your Child with Homoeopathy, Sheila Harrison, Ashgrove Press.

First-aid techniques

Your child's natural curiosity and desire to explore mean you will not be able to protect him from the occasional accident. You can avoid major catastrophes by paying special attention to home safety. You will find you develop a 'sixth sense' about danger spots outside the home, but you should always be on the lookout for potential hazards.

In the case of minor accidents all your child needs is comfort and reassurance. Minor cuts and bruises heal by themselves. A plaster on a wound does not speed healing, unless the wound is being constantly rubbed by clothing or footwear, but it can boost damaged morale and can protect an open wound from further injury.

In the case of an emergency, your prompt action could be life-saving. It is important to make yourself familiar with the techniques of first aid so that you do not have to stop and think what you should do when faced with a major accident. The guidelines below are intended to remind you, but they are no substitute for a proper first-aid course, in which you will have the opportunity to practise life-saving techniques until you can perform them automatically.

Resuscitation

It is impossible to learn how to resuscitate someone adequately from a book. It is strongly advised that you should attend a special first-aid course run by one of the first-aid organizations, in order to familiarize yourself with the necessary techniques.

Without oxygen, brain damage can rapidly set in. So if your child is not breathing you should try to resuscitate him without delay, and keep going until medical help arrives or until he starts to breathe again of his own accord.

MOUTH-TO-MOUTH RESUSCITATION FOR BABIES AND YOUNG CHILDREN

Babies and young children need a special technique of mouth-to-mouth resuscitation because of their small size. Before you begin resuscitation

If your child is involved in an accident

- Shout for help as soon as you reach the scene of the accident.
- Stay calm, and reassure your child if he is conscious.
- Avoid putting yourself in any danger. If there are hazards such as electricity, fire or water, call for help.
- Don't move your child unless strictly necessary.
- Check the three vital signs – breathing, pulse and bleeding – and deal with those (see pages 24–9) before looking for other injuries.
- Gently check your child for other injuries, disturbing him as little as possible.
- If you have not been able to summon help, call an ambulance.

Calling an ambulance
Dial 999. Be prepared to give your name and telephone number and to describe the nature of the accident and the number of people involved. The ambulance service will also need to know where you are and how to get there. If another adult is available it may be quicker to get him or her to take you to hospital by car while you sit in the back with your child and administer first aid if necessary – but not, under any circumstances, if your child is unconscious, vomiting, has multiple injuries or an airway obstruction.

you will need to check the airways (the passages between the mouth, nose and lungs). These may be blocked because fluid or vomit has collected at the back of the throat, or because the tongue is blocking the back of the mouth.

To open the airways, lie your child on a firm surface. Place a hand on his forehead and tilt his head slightly backwards (do not push too far or you may inadvertently block the air passages). Place two fingers on the end of the chin to support the jaw, then find out if your child is breathing by placing your ear close to your child's mouth and nose and listening, while noting signs such as chest movement or the feel of breath on your cheek.

If your child is breathing put him into the recovery position (see page 27) and keep an eye on him in case breathing stops. If your child is not breathing, check to see that no vomit, object or debris is blocking his airways, by running your finger around the inside of his mouth. Remove any obstruction. If your child is still not breathing begin mouth-to-mouth resuscitation at once, by following the steps below:

1. Your child should be lying on his back with his head tilted back slightly, as described above.

2. Slip a hand under his back to support him and ensure his head remains tilted.
3. Open your mouth and take a shallow breath. Make a seal over your child's mouth and nose with your lips. Puff gently into them, watching to see if his chest rises. *Do not* blow hard as you could damage his lungs.
4. Remove your mouth and let the air come out of your child's mouth and nose. As it does you should see his chest fall.
5. Repeat until your child starts breathing, using a rate of about 20 breaths a minute.
6. As soon as your child starts breathing place him on his side in the recovery position (see page 27).

IF YOUR CHILD'S HEART HAS STOPPED

If your child remains pale or his complexion becomes bluish-grey, if his pupils are enlarged, or if you cannot feel his heartbeat, his heart may have stopped. In this case you will have to perform heart massage if you have been trained to do so, as if the heart has stopped any oxygen you breathe into his body via his mouth will not be pumped to his body tissues and brain damage will set in.

To perform heart massage (external chest compression)

1. Lie your child on a firm surface. Place your arm under his head and

grasp his upper arm with your hand to support his head and back.
2. Place two fingers of your other hand midway between his nipples and press his breastbone rhythmically, depressing it about 2.5cm (1 inch).
3. For a slightly older child use the heel of your hand and press and release.
4. Continue to press and release at the rate of about five compressions to one breath of mouth-to-mouth resuscitation, blowing and pressing alternately.
5. After one minute check his pulse again, and do so at regular three-minute intervals after that.

The recovery position

This position keeps your child's airway open at the same time as making sure he does not roll on to his back or face. It helps prevent his tongue blocking his airway, and allows any fluids to drain from his mouth so he doesn't choke.

1. Turn your child halfway over on to his stomach with his underneath arm behind his body and the other arm bent slightly to support him and prevent him rolling onto his face.
2. Bend his upper leg at right angles to his body to support it and prevent him rolling over.
3. Tilt his head backwards (but not too far) so that he can breathe and to allow any fluids or vomit to drain away.

4. Stay with him while someone else calls for medical help and check at regular intervals that he is still breathing.

To check your child's heartbeat

The easiest way to do this is to check the pulse in the carotid arteries which lie in the neck. Locate your child's windpipe and slide your fingers into the groove that lies between it and the neck muscles below the jaw. Use the pads of your fingers rather than your fingertips or you could be misled by the beating of your own pulse. Continue to feel for five seconds. If you don't feel a pulse the heart has stopped.

UNCONSCIOUSNESS

Unconsciousness may be caused by head injury, electric shock, shock or a fit. The danger is that the normal reflexes do not operate if your child is unconscious, which leaves him open to the risk of choking. Never leave an unconscious child alone even for a second. If your child loses consciousness even for a moment following an injury or for any other reason he must see a doctor.

To check if a baby is unconscious tap his feet to see if there is any response.

To check if an older child is unconscious shake him gently by the shoulders and speak to him. If he responds he is conscious.

If your child or baby is unconscious check to see if he is breathing (see page 25). Make sure his airway is not obstructed and clear it if necessary (see page 25). If he is breathing, carefully examine him for the source of any injuries then put him into the recovery position (see page 27). If he is not breathing begin resuscitation measures as outlined on page 25.

Do not give your child anything to eat or drink before he receives medical help, in case he needs an operation.

BLEEDING

Bleeding may be external or internal. Internal bleeding means that blood vessels inside the body are severed, in which case there may be no visible signs of injury. Serious bleeding can lead to shock. Most minor cuts and grazes can be treated simply by washing with soap and water and applying a dressing if necessary (see page 38). To treat severe bleeding, apply pressure over the wound, using a sterile dressing or a clean piece of material to staunch bleeding. As you press, raise the injured limb above the level of the heart to stem the blood flow to the affected area. Keep pressing until bleeding stops. If the bleeding is very severe press against the wound in such a way that the blood vessel is pressed against the nearest bone. Get medical help urgently. Once bleeding has stopped, apply a dressing, pad or bandage over the wound or wrap it in the material you used to maintain pressure. Seek medical help without delay as your child will probably need stitches. If your child's skin has been punctured by something sharp, such as a piece of glass, that has stayed lodged in the skin, do not attempt to remove it. It may be preventing further bleeding.

ACCIDENTS AND INJURIES

BITES AND STINGS

Prevent the spread of infection or poison by cleaning the bitten area carefully with soap and water. Specific treatment depends on the source of the bite or sting.

ANIMAL BITES

In general, deal with dog, cat, human or other animal bites and scratches in the same way as you would any dirty wound. Wash thoroughly with soap and water to remove traces of saliva and dirt. If the skin is broken it is worth seeing a doctor. Control bleeding by covering the bite with a wad of sterile gauze. If the bleeding is heavy press some ice against the pad (not directly against the skin). Once bleeding has stopped, dress the wound with a plaster. Make sure your child's tetanus immunization is up-to-date (see page 150). Dogs and cats abroad may be carrying rabies, so always report a bite at once to the local doctor and take the name and address of the owner. Take sensible precautions with animals, and tell children not to approach strange animals.

SNAKE BITES

Snake bites are rare in this country. The only poisonous snake to live in the British Isles is the adder, which is greyish in colour with a zigzag pattern on its back. You may come across others abroad. Stay calm and reassure your child. If she is in pain give her paracetamol syrup. If your child has been bitten by an adder, or if you are unsure whether the snake is poisonous, seek medical advice. Thoroughly wash the bitten area with soapy water to remove traces of venom, then cover it with a clean dressing. Keep your child as still as possible. Make a mental note of the snake's appearance so the hospital can give appropriate treatment. Do not suck the wound or apply a tourniquet.

BEE AND WASP STINGS

These are not usually serious unless your child has been stung
repeatedly or is allergic to them. In the case of a bee sting, carefully
remove the sting if you can see it. Don't squeeze the wound as this will
inject poison further into the skin. Wash with soap and water. Apply
ice, wrapped in a cloth or flannel, to reduce swelling. Calamine lotion
or baking soda applied to the wound will help relieve pain. If your child
has been stung by a number of bees or wasps, or if she is reacting with
signs of shock – fast pulse, clammy, pale skin, breathlessness, fainting
and sweating – seek medical help at once.

JELLYFISH

Jellyfish stings are extremely painful. Wrap your hand in a cloth and
gently wipe away any tentacles, then wash the area with salt water (not
fresh water) or surgical spirit, which neutralizes jellyfish poisons. Take
your child to the doctor or to casualty if she develops symptoms of
shock.

BROKEN BONES

Children's bones are soft and springy, like a green twig, and are more
likely just to crack on one side than to break. Such 'green-stick'
fractures, as they are called, need only splinting to heal. The problem is
that it is often difficult to diagnose a break. In fact the only certain way
is by X-ray. If a child's 'bruised' arm or leg does not seem to be healing
and he is not using it normally, it could be that he has broken a bone.
Even fractures of the head may go unnoticed for a while. Other types of
break are simple fractures, in which the bone has broken in one place,
and compound fractures, in which the bone sticks through the skin.

WHAT TO LOOK OUT FOR

- Pain or tenderness over the bone or joint
- Inability to move the injured limb
- Abnormal shape, position or movement in the injured area
- Swelling or bluish discolouration over the injury

To make a sling

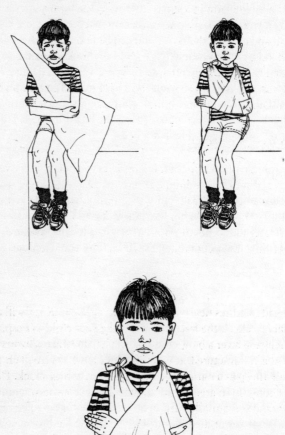

A sling can be used to support and immobilize an injured bone or joint of the arm. Use a triangular bandage or improvise one, using a scarf or piece of cloth folded into a triangle. Sit your child down and support his injured arm, placing it at right angles to his chest with the hand raised slightly higher than the elbow. Place the sling with the long edge down his body parallel to his side and the top end over his shoulder. Continuing to support his arm, bring the lower end up and tie the ends together in a reef knot above his collar bone for comfort. Bring the loose point at the elbow forward and pin or tie at the front of the sling.

ARMS AND LEGS

Support a broken arm in a sling. Improvise one from a scarf or piece of sheeting if you don't have one in your first-aid kit. The arm should be kept still and close to the body, and can be bound loosely to your child's body. Bandage a broken leg to the child's other leg. *Do not* try to straighten the arm or leg if it appears bent. Take your child to the nearest casualty unit if you suspect he has broken his arm. If your child has a broken leg do not move him. Call an ambulance.

FINGERS AND TOES

Small children often trap their fingers in car or house doors, and toes may have heavy objects dropped on them. Severe bruising is more likely than an actual break, but if you think bones might be broken take your child to hospital. Wrap the fingers or toes in a pad of cloth soaked in cold water to soothe the pain. Alternatively tape broken fingers together. If you suspect broken toes do not let your child walk.

HEAD

Most head fractures heal without treatment but an X-ray will usually be necessary to check the fracture, so do take your child to hospital.

Concussion after a blow or fall on the head is the real worry, even if the head is not fractured. It is common for a baby or small child to cry then fall asleep as a natural reaction after any sort of shock. Danger signs of concussion are: vomiting, loss of consciousness, if only for a moment, an unnaturally deep sleep with heavy or laboured breathing, and pallor. If any of these occur, call the doctor, who can decide whether your child needs to be admitted to hospital for observation.

TREATMENT

If you suspect a broken bone then take your child to hospital, where the doctor will do an X-ray to check what kind of fracture it is.

- In the case of a straightforward break the bone will be strapped with a tight bandage or set in a plaster cast until it has knitted together.
- In the case of a compound fracture your child will need a general

anaesthetic and the doctor will return the bones to their rightful place and again immobilize them with plaster.
- In the case of a very severely broken leg traction may be necessary.

Most broken bones heal within 6 to 10 weeks, depending on the severity of the fracture. Keep the plaster cast dry and help your child to enjoy life as usual within the limitations of the injury.

BRUISES

Bruises are the most common minor injuries. They can come up very quickly and be quite alarming in appearance, especially on the head, but are rarely a cause for concern.

Bruises are caused when damaged blood vessels release blood into the surrounding tissues. As the blood is broken down the bruise changes colour and fades from reddish-purple, to yellow, before fading of its own accord. Bruises are more visible on fair skin than on dark skin, and will usually fade within 10 to 14 days.

If a bruise does not heal and tenderness persists or worsens, check with the doctor to make sure no bones have been broken.

A minor bruise needs no treatment other than a hug and a kiss better. For a larger bruise apply ice wrapped in a cloth to reduce swelling, and raise the bruised part above the level of the heart for 15 minutes. If the bruise remains tender after 24 hours, applying warm, wet compresses will help speed healing.

BURNS

Treatment varies according to the type of burn, and all but the most superficial burns should be seen by the doctor. When treating a burn your aim should be to soothe pain, prevent shock and avoid the injury becoming infected. Electrical burns are especially serious because they appear minor but are in fact often deep.

SUPERFICIAL BURNS

Red skin with mild swelling and pain. These burns affect only the top layer of skin, and though they are intensely painful, healing is usually quick. Sunburn, or brief contact with something hot, such as a kettle, saucepan, or iron, are common causes. The best treatment is to immerse the burn in cold water or under the tap for 10 minutes to clean and cool the skin. Do not apply butter or other household remedies as they are not effective and could be a source of infection. Cover the burn with a piece of clean, dry cloth or a sterile dressing. Give your child paracetamol syrup to ease pain. Seek medical attention for a burn that blisters.

DEEP BURNS

These affect deeper layers of skin, causing them to leak body fluids which then form blisters. The skin is red, streaked or blotchy, and there is swelling, blistering and pain. Such burns may be caused by scalding with hot liquids and steam, or may be a result of severe sunburn. Cool and cover the burn as described above then take your child to hospital. Do not attempt to remove clothes over a deep burn.

CHEMICAL BURNS

Put on a pair of waterproof gloves and wash off the chemical with plenty of cold water. If the chemical is on your child's clothing remove his clothes as they will continue to burn him. But do not attempt to remove clothes that have stuck to the skin. Seek medical advice, even if the burn is small.

FULL-THICKNESS BURNS

This means the deeper layers of skin have been burnt. Because nerve endings have been destroyed there may be little or no pain. The skin is white and charred. These burns are usually caused by fire or electric shock, and may form the centre of a more superficial burn, making them difficult to detect. Shock is the biggest risk, and medical attention is vital. If your child has suffered an electric shock (see page 40), break the current by switching it off or moving him away from the source of electricity with a broom handle or other non-conductive object. Remove or loosen clothing. If the burn covers a large area put your child in a cool bath. For smaller burns put the burnt area under a cold running tap or in a sink of cold water (do not use ice) or apply cold wet flannels for five minutes. Gently pat dry and cover with a clean dry cloth or dressing. Take the child to the casualty department or call an ambulance.

DOS AND DON'TS

- Don't burst blisters.
- Don't apply ointment, antiseptic, butter or other home remedies.
- Don't press on the burnt area.
- Don't remove clothing that has stuck to the burnt area.
- Don't use cotton wool or any fluffy material such as lint to cover a burn.
- Do seek medical attention at once for all but the most minor burns.

If your child's clothing has caught fire

If your child's clothes have caught fire try and put him on the floor, as flames rise upwards. Smother the flames with a heavy, non-flammable item such as a coat, blanket, rug or thick towel. Don't use anything synthetic as this will melt and burn him still further. If nothing is available throw yourself on top of him, making sure that you cover him completely as any pockets of air will feed the flames and could set your own clothing alight. If you have a bucket or bowl of water handy you could throw this over him to quench the flames, but don't do this if electricity is involved.

Once you have smothered the fire call an ambulance. Do not remove any burnt clothing that has adhered to your child's skin.

CHOKING

Coughing is the body's mechanism for ridding itself of a foreign body in the air passages. If your child is coughing or crying, don't rush to do anything but watch her carefully in case she needs your help.

If your child can only cough faintly or is gasping for breath or turning blue it is an emergency.

FOR BABIES UNDER ONE YEAR

If your baby is choking but can breathe, cry or cough, stand by ready to help but don't do anything yet. Her own coughing is more effective than anything you can do. If your baby stops breathing try the following steps.

1. Lie the baby face down on your forearm with her head sloping downwards.
2. Give four rapid blows between the shoulder blades using the heel of your hand.
3. Turn the baby over so she is face up with her head still lower than her body.
4. Place two fingertips on her chest between the nipples and press firmly and rapidly four times.
5. If she continues to choke repeat this sequence until the object is dislodged.
6. If she stops breathing give mouth-to-mouth resuscitation (see page 24).

BABIES AND TODDLERS OVER ONE YEAR

If your child has been eating or playing with a small object then suddenly collapses, grasps her throat and wheezes or coughs, suspect choking as the cause. If she cannot speak:

1. Stand behind her and bend her forwards so her head is between her knees, then strike her four times sharply between the shoulder blades.
2. If she continues to choke put both arms around her from behind and press your fist against her abdomen.
3. With your other hand press on your fist and give four sharp inward and upward thrusts.
4. Continue until the object is coughed up and your child begins to breath normally.
5. If she becomes unconscious begin mouth-to-mouth resuscitation (see page 24).

DOS AND DON'TS

- Do keep all small objects out of reach of your child.
- Don't give your child large play things with small, loose or removable parts.
- Never leave your child alone when she is eating.
- Don't give peanuts or other small, hard foods to a child under three.

CUTS AND GRAZES

Small cuts and grazes can be treated simply at home, so long as they are not gaping or bleeding freely (in which case there is the risk of shock), are not causing numbness or inability to move, and do not hurt when the child moves. A very deep cut, or a cut in which an object such as a nail or a large sliver of glass or wood has become embedded in the skin, needs medical attention. Such wounds carry a greater risk of tetanus than small, superficial scrapes or cuts.

FOR MINOR CUTS, SCRAPES OR SPLINTERS

1. Wash the wound thoroughly with soap and water.
2. Remove any particles of gravel or surface splinters. Do not attempt to remove deeply embedded objects.
3. Rinse with clean running water and pat dry gently.
4. If the edges of the cut are gaping hold them together and apply a narrow strip of adhesive tape.
5. If the cut fails to heal or you notice tenderness, pus, redness and swelling, or red streaks leading from it, especially if your child has swollen glands and seems unwell, contact the doctor at once, as this is a sign that infection has set in.

SEEK MEDICAL HELP IF

- The wound is dirty.
- There are any objects embedded in it such as glass or dirt.
- The wound bleeds heavily or is very deep or long.
- The wound has jagged edges.
- The wound is deep but has only a small puncture hole.
- Your child was playing in a dirty area, for example in soil where there is contamination from farm animals.
- The wound was caused by a dirty object such as a rusty nail or tin.

The doctor will clean and stitch the wound if necessary. Facial injuries will probably be stitched to avoid scarring. If your child has not had a tetanus injection he will be given one. An antibiotic dressing or medication may be prescribed to fight off any infection that may have entered the wound.

DOS AND DON'TS

- Do choose the right shape and size of dressing for the wound. Select a dressing that is large enough to cover the wound but that does not hinder movement.
- Do cover wounds if they are in areas that are likely to get knocked, injured again, or dirty. Very minor cuts and scrapes heal better if exposed to the air.
- If you use a dressing do change it every day.
- Do examine the wound for signs of infection every time you change the dressing (see above).
- Don't put adhesive on the wound itself as it will be painful.
- When the time comes to remove the adhesive dressing soak it in a little baby oil or any other oil to lessen pain as you pull it off.

DROWNING

A child can drown in as little as 5cm (2 inches) of water. If your child has fallen into shallow water there is a risk of neck or back injury – be careful not to bend her neck or allow her to make sudden movements.

If your child is drowning, pay attention to your own safety while attempting to rescue her. Do not jump into the water yourself unless there is no alternative. Reach out with your hand, a pole, towel, rope or life belt if there is one available. If you have to swim out to her, take a board or towel for her to hold on to, in order to avoid her grabbing you and pulling you under in her panic.

Start artificial respiration immediately (see below). Don't waste time trying to empty water from her lungs.

If your child has been immersed in cold water for a long time there is a danger of hypothermia (cold injury).

If your child is not breathing, start mouth-to-mouth resuscitation (see page 24). You should start this while still in the water and continue on land until she starts breathing and you can feel her pulse. Don't give up, even if she appears lifeless. Cold slows down the body processes and survival is possible even after long submersion.

If your child is breathing, or once she starts breathing, lie her on her side in the recovery position (see page 27). Take her into a warm room, or cover her with a coat or blanket to keep her warm. If she is conscious take off wet clothing before covering her. If not, do not

remove wet clothing. You may give her a warm drink but don't give her
anything alcoholic.

Call an ambulance so as to get your child to the nearest casualty unit
as quickly as you can. Meanwhile sit with her and give her artificial
resuscitation if necessary.

EAR PROBLEMS

Injury to the outer ear will cause profuse bleeding even if it is only a
minor wound. Hold a clean pad to the wound and treat as you would
any cut.

FOREIGN BODIES IN THE EAR

Insects occasionally become trapped in the ear, and young children
may put small objects such as nuts or beads in the ear, where they
become lodged. If you can remove the object easily with a pair of
tweezers, do so gently. But don't poke the tweezers or anything else
down the ear. Take your child to the doctor to make sure there are no
fragments left inside.

Your child may be able to dislodge a small hard object such as a pea
or bead by shaking his head, with the affected ear downwards. Do not
hit his head. If shaking his head doesn't work see the doctor.

If a live insect is trapped in your child's ear drip a few drops of
almond or baby oil into the ear to kill it, then let the doctor remove it.
Do not pour oil or water over other objects as they may cause the object
to swell, making removal more difficult.

ELECTRIC SHOCK

When treating electric shock the first priority is to break the electric
contact by switching off the main circuit breaker or fuse for the whole
house. Turning off the appliance is not sufficient, as only one or two
wires are controlled by the switch.

If you cannot turn off the electricity, stand on a dry insulating
material such as a folded newspaper or a rubber door mat and use a
non-conductive object such as a wooden broom handle to push your

child off the wire or the wire off her. *Do not* use anything metal or stand on anything wet, as these conduct electricity. If the child is lying in anything liquid take care not to tread in it for the same reason.

Call an ambulance, and in the meantime if your child is not breathing begin artificial resuscitation at once (see page 24) and continue for as long as necessary.

If your child is unconscious but breathing place her on her side in the recovery position (see page 27). Cover her lightly with a blanket or clothing.

Treat any burns as described on page 34.

DOS AND DON'TS

- Do remain calm and careful to ensure you are not electrocuted yourself.
- Do separate your child from the source of electricity before taking other measures.
- Don't put butter, ointment or pain-relief sprays on burns.
- Don't put pressure on any burns or allow your child to walk on any.
- Don't remove clothing that has stuck to a burn.

EYE INJURIES

If a foreign body has entered the eye it will water and appear red. Your child may complain of stinging or burning when he blinks and be reluctant to open his eye. Examine the eye closely in a good light. Natural watering will often be sufficient to flush out the object but if not, gently flush the eye with water. If this does not remove a visible object, cover the eye with a clean pad or handkerchief and tape it into place. Seek medical advice.

If you cannot see the object, gently pull down the lower lid and examine the inner surface. If you then see the object use the twisted end of a clean handkerchief or cotton wool bud to remove it.

To check the upper eyelid lay a cotton wool bud or matchstick across the top of the lid (a) and fold the lid up over it (b); then either flush the eye with lukewarm water or remove the object with a cotton wool bud or the end of a clean handkerchief as before. If your child's eyes continue to water after the object has been dislodged or if he complains

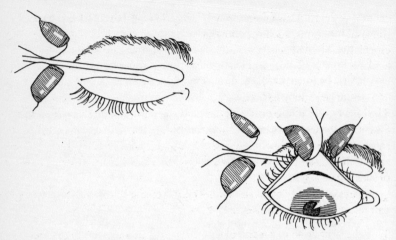

of pain or blurred vision, take him to the doctor, as the surface of the eye may be scratched. *If the foreign body is embedded in the eye*, or if a cinder has entered the eye, do not try to remove it. Do not rub or press on the eye. Close both your child's eyes and cover with a pad taped loosely in place. Take your child to the doctor at once.

BLACK EYE

A black eye looks alarming but it is rarely serious. Apply a cold compress to reduce swelling and ease pain.

CHEMICAL SPLASHES

If your child has splashed a stinging liquid such as a corrosive chemical in his eye, flush the eye immediately with cold water, letting the water run from the inner corner outwards to avoid the chemical getting into the unaffected eye. Do not let your child rub his eye. Continue the flushing for 10 minutes, then apply a clean cloth pad and tape loosely into place. Seek medical help immediately.

HYPOTHERMIA

Hypothermia (when the body temperature drops below 35°C/95°F can result from exposure to extreme cold either outside or indoors, and may occur if your child has fallen into cold water. Hypothermia slows down the vital functions, such as heart, kidneys, lungs and so on. Babies are especially at risk because they move around less to keep warm and because their bodies are less efficient at regulating temperature, so you should not leave your baby in an unheated room in cold weather.

Signs of hypothermia include drowsiness, confusion and weakness. The child's skin is pale or bluish but her extremities may be bright pink. She will appear shivery and her skin will feel cold to the touch. A baby suffering hypothermia will have a cold skin, and may not cry; she will appear drowsy and limp, and if you try to feed her will only be capable of sucking weakly.

Always carry out any warming procedures gradually as sudden heat can result in further heat loss and shock.

1. Take your child to a warm place (if you are outdoors find the nearest shelter).
2. Remove any wet clothing and wrap your child in a blanket or towel. A layer of aluminium foil wrapped over this will help keep heat in. Alternatively cuddle your child next to your own body.
3. Give her a warm (not hot) drink and call the doctor. If you have a thermometer take your child's temperature at regular intervals, and if it does not start to rise call an ambulance.

MOUTH INJURIES

When crawlers and toddlers fall they often cut their lips or bite their tongue or inner cheek. Such injuries may bleed profusely but are rarely serious. Stay calm and reassure your child.

Staunch bleeding by placing a wad of gauze or a clean, folded handkerchief on both sides of the cut to close it and hold for 10 minutes. If the cut looks jagged or is large or gaping, seek medical attention as it will probably need stitches. If a tooth has been knocked out wrap it in a clean, wet handkerchief and take the child and the tooth to the dentist, who may be able to re-implant it.

POISONING

If you suspect your child has swallowed something poisonous act immediately; do not wait for symptoms to develop.

Call your local casualty unit or your doctor and be ready to tell them what kind of poison has been swallowed, how much, and when. Describe any symptoms and any treatment you may have given. The casualty unit or your doctor will usually be able to tell you what steps you can take while waiting for the ambulance or while being driven to the hospital.

Take the poison container or a sample of any leaves or berries with you for examination or testing. If your child has eaten part of a plant, take enough with you to enable it to be identified. If your child has eaten some pills or swallowed a household chemical, take the container even if it is empty. If your child has vomited, take the vomited material with you for testing. If your child has swallowed pills, the doctor will want to know how many were vomited up.

If you are sure that your child has not swallowed a corrosive chemical (see list below), induce vomiting by sticking a finger in the back of her throat. If your child is becoming unconscious, or if she is having a fit or appears confused, *do not* make her vomit.

If your child has taken a corrosive poison *do not* make her sick, as the vomit will burn her again as it comes up. Give her sips of cold water or milk and get her to hospital immediately.

If your child is unconscious call an ambulance and give first aid while waiting for it to arrive. Place your child in the recovery position (see page 27), check her breathing and if necessary give mouth-to-mouth resuscitation (see page 25), being especially careful not to get any poison in your own mouth.

DO NOT MAKE YOUR CHILD VOMIT IF SHE HAS SWALLOWED

- Ammonia
- Bleach
- Corn or wart remover
- Dishwasher detergent
- Drain or toilet cleaner
- Metal polish
- Floor polish or wax
- Furniture polish or wax
- Petrol
- Paraffin
- Lighter fluid
- Liquid naphtha

- Oven cleaner
- Quicklime
- Rust remover
- Pills used by diabetics to test the urine

- Paint thinner
- Turpentine
- Wood preservative

Shock

Shock is a condition that occurs if the blood pressure becomes lowered following a loss of blood or other body fluids or if the heart has been affected by an accident, with the result that the vital organs are deprived of blood. Shock may be caused by severe bleeding or burns, electric shock, dehydration following diarrhoea and vomiting, or as an allergic reaction to a bee sting or certain types of medication. Signs of shock include quick, shallow breathing, a weak, rapid pulse, a pale or bluish face, giddiness or sickness, sweating, dizziness, blurred vision, restlessness, extreme thirst and unconsciousness.

Stay calm and reassure your child. If he has been injured, give any necessary first aid but move him as little as possible.

Lie your child on a blanket and raise his legs higher than his heart, supporting them on cushions. Loosen any tight clothing. Keep him warm by covering him with a blanket or clothing, but do not use hot-water bottles, an electric blanket, or anything that will raise his body temperature too quickly and divert blood to the surface of the skin away from the vital organs.

Do not give your child a hot drink, in case he needs an anaesthetic for his injuries.

If your child is unconscious put him in the recovery position (see page 27) and watch him to make sure he is still breathing.

Ring a doctor straight away.

Splinters

Most splinters can be removed quite simply at home, with the exception of shards of glass which should be removed by a doctor. Wood splinters are the most common. Try to get hold of the end of the splinter with tweezers and pull it out slowly so it does not break.

If the splinter is under the surface of the skin take a sharp, fine needle and sterilize it by standing it in some antiseptic for a few minutes. Numb the skin with an ice cube then gently break the surface with the needle to expose the splinter. It should now be possible to remove it with a pair of tweezers.

Wash the area with soap and water and apply an antiseptic cream. A plaster should not be necessary.

Consult the doctor or attend casualty if the splinter is very deep or large, if it is made of glass, if it has come from something dirty, or if you cannot remove it easily.

SPRAIN

A sprain is a stretched or torn ligament (the tendon that supports a joint and limits its movement). It usually occurs when a sudden movement wrenches the joint, causing bleeding into the joint which in turn causes swelling and bruising. Ankles, knees and wrists are the areas most susceptible to sprains. They are unusual in very young children whose joints are supple. It is not always possible to tell the difference between a sprain and a fracture, so an X-ray will usually be necessary to determine the nature of the injury.

To treat a sprain, raise the injured limb and apply cold compresses to reduce swelling. Wrap a crêpe bandage around the limb, making sure it is not too tight. Encourage your child to rest for a day or so.

If the limb is very painful, or if it is in an abnormal shape or position, go to the casualty department as it could be broken. Consult your doctor if, after two days, the swelling has not gone down or the child is still in severe pain and cannot bear his weight on the affected area.

SUFFOCATION

Babies and children do occasionally manage to pull plastic bags over their heads. If you discover your child in this sort of difficulty, or trapped under some heavy covering, remove the cause. If your child begins to breathe normally stay calm and reassure her. If not begin artificial resuscitation (see page 24) at once and call an ambulance.

Part II

A–Z OF CHILDHOOD ILLNESSES

ABDOMINAL PAIN

Pain in the abdomen (stomach ache) is one of the commonest childhood symptoms. It can be caused by something trivial or it can be the first sign of something more serious. So long as the pain is not accompanied by other symptoms such as diarrhoea and/or vomiting, weight loss, pain on urinating, blood in the motions or other obvious signs of illness, the cause is likely to be unimportant.

Small children are often unable to identify the source of their discomfort and so may complain of 'tummy ache' when in fact the problem is something else entirely, such as a middle ear infection. Some infections, such as tonsillitis, cause swelling of the glands throughout the body. Some children are unable to distinguish nausea from stomach ache.

A sudden severe attack of stomach ache can be alarming for your child and you. It can be difficult to distinguish between minor causes and those which are serious, and if in doubt you should not hesitate to contact the doctor.

SEE THE DOCTOR IF:

- Abdominal pain is accompanied by a raised temperature, loss of appetite, diarrhoea and/or vomiting, or blood in the motions, or if your child appears listless and generally ill.
- The pain is so severe that your child cannot be distracted from it.
- The pain lasts longer than four hours.
- Your child experiences discomfort on passing urine.
- The pain is very severe or becomes worse, or if it becomes continuous after having been intermittent.

HOW TO TREAT ABDOMINAL PAIN

- Treatment will depend on the cause of the pain. You can help by staying calm and reassuring your child.
- Do not treat stomach pain with pain relievers or over-the-counter antacids or laxatives. These could mask symptoms or be positively dangerous in some cases.

RECURRENT ABDOMINAL PAIN

Some children regularly complain of stomach ache, despite being
apparently fit and well. Recurrent abdominal pain is less common in
pre-school-age children than in those over five. Nonetheless it can
happen. No one quite knows what is the cause of this type of stomach
pain, but it is often associated with stress and anxiety. It is thought that
some children are hypersensitive to the workings of their own insides,
especially when they are tense for some reason. They interpret as
painful the normal waves of contractions that occur as food passes
through the gut.

HOW TO TREAT RECURRENT ABDOMINAL PAIN

- If your child complains of recurrent abdominal pains it is important
  to recognize that they are real and not just in her mind.
- See the doctor to rule out possible physical causes for your child's
  discomfort.
- Keep a diary of when your child suffers stomach pain – it could be
  associated with food she has eaten, in which case you might suspect
  food allergy. Alternatively you may notice certain patterns – for
  instance she may always get a stomach ache on the day she has to go
  to toddler group. Once you have tracked down possible sources of
  anxiety you will be able to help your child cope with any stresses in
  her life.

See also: Appendicitis; Colic; Constipation; Intussusception.

ACNE, NEONATAL

Acne is the skin's reaction to any sort of hormonal upheaval. In the
case of new babies it occurs as a result of the stimulation of the skin
follicles by the hormone androgen, which is passed on to your baby
during pregnancy. Any time during the first six months of your baby's
life his skin may come out in whitish-yellow spots, especially in greasy
areas such as around the nose.

HOW TO TREAT NEONATAL ACNE

- As the hormone passes from your baby's system the blocked pores will clear of their own accord with no further treatment. Occasionally your doctor may prescribe benzoyl peroxide, a special cream or ointment, if the acne does not seem to be clearing up.
- Wash your baby's skin gently and pat dry twice a day.
- Make sure any flannels you use on your baby's skin are kept scrupulously clean.

ALLERGIES

Allergies are detected more frequently nowadays, and it's thought that one in five children suffers from some sort of allergy. The word allergy simply means an altered reaction. This can be in the form of a headache, vomiting, rashes, migraine or wheeziness. Allergies can be provoked by food, house dust, cat or dog hair, skin scales, or fumes in the atmosphere. Common allergens include wheat, milk and some forms of antibiotics.

What usually happens is that the first time your child comes into contact with the substance to which she is allergic there is no reaction. But this first exposure leads to antibodies being formed, and later when she meets the allergen again she has an allergic response. For instance, you may give your child strawberries for the first time one week and think she loves them, only to be faced with a rash the next time she eats them. The allergic response is the body's way of trying to fight off the invader.

Allergies tend to run in families, so if you or your husband are prone to hay fever, asthma, or other illnesses, then your child may well have the same problem. Don't automatically jump to the conclusion that your child is suffering from an allergy. Take her to the doctor for a check-up and don't put her on an exclusion diet without consulting the doctor. Thankfully many children grow out of allergies, so make sure that you stay in contact with your doctor so your child's allergic reactions can be challenged from time to time. However, if your child has a tendency towards being allergic, you may find that she grows out of her eczema only to come down with asthma or some other allergy.

WHAT TO LOOK OUT FOR

- Wheezing
- Vomiting
- Stomach cramps
- Diarrhoea
- Eczema
- Rashes
- Runny nose

- Catarrh
- Itchy or watery eyes
- Pallid skin with dark rings around the eyes
- Swelling
- Possible behaviour problems, such as hyperactivity

HOW TO TREAT ALLERGIES

- There are two medical lines of approach. Your doctor may prescribe creams, ointments or drugs to ease the symptoms of the allergy. There is also a technique called desensitization, which involves tracking down the source of the allergy by special tests and giving a course of injections of the offending substance until the body is able to cope with it. However, this is seldom used on children and then only in a specialist clinic.
- Try to avoid exposing your child to the causes of her allergy. For example, if house dust is a problem, always vacuum rather than sweeping; dampen the dust, and keep your child out of her room while you are cleaning it.
- Don't fuss. Treat your child in a matter-of-fact way, and don't make her feel 'different'.
- Make sure other people with whom your child spends time know about the allergy, e.g. relatives, friends, toddler group organizer, childminder.
- If your child is allergic to a particular food or additive and she is invited to a party, send a note to the person who is holding the party, explaining the problem.
- Avoid undue stress or excitement, as these can often spark off an attack.
- Do all you can to keep your child comfortable when she is suffering an attack, e.g. cool bathing for itchy rashes.

For advice and support contact: Action Against Allergy, 43 The Downs, London SW20 8HG. Tel: 01-947 5082.
National Society for Research into Allergy, P.O. Box 45, Hinckley, Leicestershire LE10 1JY.

See also: Asthma; Bronchitis; Eczema; Hay fever; Hives; Rashes, Bites and stings (listed under Accidents and Injuries).

ANAEMIA

Anaemia is a shortage or abnormality of oxygen-carrying red blood cells in the body. The main causes are a lack of iron in the diet, blood loss, some infections, a few rare conditions affecting newborn babies, and one or two blood diseases in which the red blood cells are destroyed. If you carried your baby to full term he will have been born with approximately six months' supply of iron. Premature babies lack their full quota because of their shorter time in the womb, and twins may also be short of iron because of having to share their supply. In these cases your baby will usually be prescribed special iron drops or medicine.

If a toddler becomes anaemic it is most likely as a result of his eating an unbalanced diet due to food faddiness, or because his diet is otherwise restricted in some way. In this case the doctor will probably give you advice on diet, plus some iron medicine. Very rarely, a blood transfusion is needed.

WHAT TO LOOK OUT FOR

- Paleness especially around the eye rims, lips, fingernails and tongue
- Undue tiredness
- Breathlessness
- Loss of appetite
- Irritability
- Rapid pulse
- Severe lack of energy
- Occasional food cravings

HOW TO TREAT ANAEMIA

- To prevent or treat anaemia make sure your child's diet is rich in iron. Suitable foods include: meat, especially liver, kidney, heart and so on; fish, especially dark, oily fish such as mackerel, herrings, sardines; dark green vegetables such as broccoli, kale, cabbage; nuts, dried apricots, sesame seeds, egg yolk. Contrary to popular opinion, spinach is not a good source of iron because it contains a substance that blocks the uptake of iron by the body. Vitamin C helps the

absorption of iron by the system; so make sure your child eats an
orange or drinks orange juice with his meals.
- If you suspect your child is anaemic, seek medical advice. Very
occasionally it can be an indication of something more serious.
- Breast-feed if you can for the first four to six months of your baby's
life, as this encourages the uptake of iron in the system.
- Keep all iron medicines out of reach of children.

See also: Jaundice; Leukaemia; Sickle-cell anaemia; Thalassaemia.

ANAL FISSURE

This is a split in the lining of your child's back passage, which usually
results from constipation. If you notice fresh blood on your child's
nappy or knickers it is probably a result of an anal fissure, though you
should always see the doctor in case the bleeding indicates more serious
problems. Your child will find it extremely painful to open her bowels
and may start to hold back her bowel motions, with the result that she
becomes constipated again, thus creating a vicious circle.

HOW TO TREAT ANAL FISSURE

- Prevent the problem occurring by making sure your child does not
became constipated. Give her a wholefood diet with plenty of fruit
and vegetables and lots of fluids.
- Consult your doctor, who will probably prescribe a soothing
ointment and may suggest a gentle laxative until the fissure has
healed.
- Hot baths will help soothe the pain.

See also: Constipation.

APPENDICITIS

The appendix is a small tube that leads off the gut, to the lower right
side of the abdomen. Because it is a dead end, if it becomes blocked
bacteria multiply and make the appendix inflamed. If left, it is liable to
burst, resulting in peritonitis and infecting the whole abdomen. It used

to be thought that the appendix was totally redundant, and doctors would often remove it purely to prevent appendicitis occurring. Today it is believed that the appendix may play some part in the immune system.

Appendicitis is difficult to diagnose, especially in a small child. It is extremely rare in babies. The pain may start around the navel and spread to the lower right side. It may be continuous, or stop and start over a period of hours. If, after examining your child gently for pain and tenderness, the doctor suspects that he has appendicitis, he or she will probably advise that your child be kept in hospital under observation until such time as a definite diagnosis is possible. This is because other illnesses, such as a urine infection and even tonsillitis or pneumonia, may produce similar symptoms to appendicitis.

WHAT TO LOOK OUT FOR

- Abdominal pain which worsens over the course of several hours, starting around the navel and spreading to the lower right-hand side
- Loss of appetite
- Vomiting
- A temperature of 37–38°C (98.6–100.4°F)
- Diarrhoea or constipation
- Tenderness in the affected area

HOW TO TREAT APPENDICITIS

- Contact the doctor immediately if you suspect appendicitis. Don't be afraid of being wrong. A doctor will never begrudge being called out on a false alarm for a small child, and delay could be dangerous.
- *Don't* give your child a laxative if he is constipated; this could make the condition worse and cause the appendix to burst.
- If appendicitis is suspected, keep your child off food and drink in case he needs an operation.
- Take your child's temperature every two hours, and check his abdomen for signs of tenderness.
- If your child has to go into hospital try to stay with him.
- If he does have his appendix out don't worry. Recovery is rapid once the source of the trouble has been removed.
- Once your child returns home make sure he has plenty of fluids,

fresh fruit and vegetables, and wholemeal cereals, to avoid strain on his digestive system.
- Help him to take it easy for a couple of weeks or so – no strenuous exercise or overexcitement.

See also: Abdominal pain; Constipation; Diarrhoea; Urine infection.

ASTHMA

An estimated 5 to 10 per cent of children suffer from asthma, a condition in which the linings of the breathing tubes become inflamed, narrowed and blocked with mucus, causing the muscles to go into spasm. It is very frightening for both you and your child if she is fighting for breath, so it is important for you to stay calm and know what action to take if your child has an attack.

Asthma can be sparked off by an allergy to dust, pollen, food or food additives, some drugs, animal fur and feathers. Exercise, overexcitement, stress, and changes in temperature can all trigger an attack. The disease tends to run in families, and a child who has asthma often has a tendency to other allergies such as eczema and hay fever. It can occur at any age, but it is difficult in a child under three to distinguish true asthma from the wheezing of chronic bronchitis. Some children suffer one attack and no more. But if your child suffers more than two attacks in a year the doctor will suspect asthma.

WHAT TO LOOK OUT FOR

- Difficulty breathing, especially breathing out
- Wheezing
- Breathlessness
- Ache in the chest
- Problems sleeping
- Raised temperature
- Runny or blocked nose
- Dry cough
- Tight chest
- Blue tinge around the mouth
- Bouts of sneezing

Living with asthma

- Don't let your child's asthma rule your life. Take all sensible precautions to prevent attacks and then treat her like an ordinary child. You may feel the urge to overprotect her. Try to resist it so she won't feel like an invalid. In this way, though her illness may occasionally stop her keeping up with other children, at least she will not feel that she is the odd one out.
- You may be able to prevent an attack occurring by being on the lookout for warning signs, such as sneezing or a runny nose. If you can stifle these early symptoms, for example by using an anti-histamine prescribed by your doctor, you may be able to fend off an attack before it starts.
- If your doctor has not managed to find what substances trigger off an attack, be alert to signs yourself. For example, your child may have attacks in a particular place, at a particular time of day, or in a particular season. Asthmatic children often benefit from being by the sea.
- Protect your child from anything you know provokes wheezing. For instance, if she is allergic to fur, give the family pet away to a good home, or compromise by keeping the pet confined to one room in the house. If you are visiting people who own an animal, either meet elsewhere or ask them to keep the animal outside during your visit.
- Go through your house and rid it of anything that harbours dust (the house-dust mite is a common allergen). Vacuum carpets regularly. Dampen dust before cleaning. Use roller blinds rather than curtains or Venetian blinds, which act as dust traps.
- Take especial care in your child's room. Keep it scrupulously dust-free. Cover the mattress with a close-fitting plastic cover. Replace blankets and feather pillows with a synthetic duvet and foam pillows.
- Your child may benefit from humid air, in which case you can buy a vaporizer to put in her room. Alternatively she may feel better if the air is cool. Try both and see which works best.
- Make sure all members of the family are aware of your child's condition and how to keep it under control.
- In very severe cases a physiotherapist will show you how to position your child chest downwards to help drain mucus from her airways. Breathing exercises for use during an attack may also help.
- Try not to let your child become overweight, as her lungs will have to work harder.
- Make sure you keep a good supply of prescribed medications, and be sure everyone who is likely to be left in charge of your child knows where to find them.
- Exercise such as swimming or walking may benefit your child, but anything too strenuous may trigger an attack.

For advice and support contact: Asthma Research Council and Asthma Society, 300 Upper Street, Islington, London N1 2XX. Tel: 01-226 2260.

HOW TO TREAT ASTHMA

- Take your child to the doctor if it is her first attack or if congestion is stopping her from eating or sleeping. You should also consult the doctor if the normally clear, whitish mucus changes to yellow or green, or is tinged with blood.
- Medical treatment is aimed at preventing and treating attacks. Prevention consists of prescribing drugs, either in the form of syrup or tablets for under-threes, or by means of a special 'spinhaler', which the child uses to breathe in the drug in powder form, for older children. Taken daily, these drugs help prevent attacks developing, and cut down the need for other medicines.
- The doctor will also prescribe special drugs called bronchodilators, which open up the airways. The drugs are usually inhaled through a variety of different types of inhaler or, for younger children who find it hard to manage using an aerosol, taken in syrup form. These drugs can also be used to ward off an attack, for instance if they are taken before a bout of exercise.
- If these steps do not succeed, the doctor may prescribe a steroid, which is inhaled or occasionally taken in tablet form.
- Stay with your child during an attack. If the attack occurs at night support her on pillows. Try to distract her with toys and games. Give her plenty to drink (drinks should not be too hot or cold). Follow any instructions given by your doctor for dealing with an attack.

BALANITIS

Balanitis is inflammation and infection under the foreskin of the penis. The foreskin reddens and swells, and your child experiences pain or burning on passing water. Sometimes there is a discharge of pus. It can occur as a result of nappy rash, a tight foreskin (which is normal up to the age of five or so) or, very rarely, diabetes. It may also be caused if your child is allergic to the soap powder you use.

WHAT TO LOOK OUT FOR

- Swollen red foreskin

- Crying or complaints of pain when passing urine
- Pus

HOW TO TREAT BALANITIS

- Keep your child's penis clean and give him a warm bath every day. *Don't* try to draw back the foreskin of a child under five.
- If your child has nappy rash, expose his bottom to the air and treat the rash with a medicated cream.
- If you suspect the soap powder you are using is causing the problem, change to one that is enzyme free and labelled for sensitive skins.
- See the doctor if the problem does not clear up. Your doctor may ask for a urine sample from your child, and/or prescribe antibiotics to clear up any infection.
- If your child suffers repeated infections, causing scarring, then circumcision may be needed when he is five or six.

BEDWETTING

Most children become dry at night between the ages of two and three, but this varies a lot and 1 in 10 children is still wetting the bed by the age of five. Undue stress or excitement may also provoke bedwetting in a child who has been previously dry. Boys and first-born children are more prone to wetting the bed than girls and subsequent children.

HOW TO TREAT BEDWETTING

- Don't worry – virtually all children grow out of it eventually.
- Make life easier for yourself by covering your child's mattress with a plastic cover and using a synthetic duvet that can be easily washed. A tumble dryer makes daily bedding washes easier.
- Don't fuss about it or your child may become tense, which will only perpetuate the problem.
- Expect the occasional wet bed up to the age of seven, especially in times of stress.
- Keep your child in nappies if possible.
- If your child is still not dry by the age of six, try incentives such as a star chart. This involves sticking a star on a chart for every dry

night. When your child has acquired seven in a row, reward her with a small treat.

- If bedwetting is getting you down, or if your child starts wetting the bed again for no obvious reason after previously being dry, consult the doctor or health visitor. There are various types of alarms and buzzer systems that wake the child when he has wet the bed – and these are very successful.

See also: Diabetes; Urinary infection.

BIRTHMARKS

Most birthmarks disappear by the age of five, and unless the birthmark is really disfiguring or widespread, there is no need to do anything.

WHAT TO LOOK OUT FOR

There are several different types of birthmark:

Strawberry mark
- A raised, red mark
- Grows larger for several months but will eventually disappear altogether before school age
- More common in girls than boys

Stork bite
- Small, reddish mark found on the back of the neck, eyelids or bridge of the nose
- Disappears eventually

Mongolian spot
- Blackish-blue, bruised appearance
- Found on the lower back or buttocks
- Usually affects dark-skinned children
- Disappears eventually

Port-wine stain
- Red patch that may cover much of the face or forehead
- May fade, but never disappears completely

Mole

- Round, brown, raised or flat mark
- Permanent

HOW TO TREAT BIRTHMARKS

- Treatment is not necessary unless the mark is of an unsightly permanent nature.
- Simple moles are harmless but see your doctor if it changes colour, bleeds or gets bigger.
- Treatment options for permanent moles usually involve camouflage make-up, which your doctor can prescribe on the NHS. Discuss this with your doctor.
- Never discuss your child's birthmark in front of him or make him self-conscious about it in any way.

BLISTER

A blister is a fluid-filled pad which is formed in order to protect damaged skin while it heals. The damage may have been initially caused by a burn, friction or chemical irritation, or occasionally by chicken pox or eczema. Blisters are commonly caused by new shoes rubbing the back of the heel.

WHAT TO LOOK OUT FOR

- Raised area of skin containing fluid

HOW TO TREAT A BLISTER

- Small blisters usually heal up with no trouble, unless they burst or become infected.
- Leave blisters alone. Don't try to burst one. If the blister is in an awkward spot, protect it with a dressing to prevent it bursting accidentally. Once burst they become very painful.
- If other symptoms develop, such as a rash or itching, take your child to see the doctor, as the blister could herald the start of chicken pox.
- See the doctor if the blister becomes red, swollen or tender, or if it is

caused by a burn, is very large, or becomes pussy. Red streaks extending into the surrounding skin are an indication that the blister has become infected and the infection is spreading through the blood. See a doctor at once.

- When your child has new shoes take special care to make sure they fit properly, and ease them into use gradually.

BOILS

A boil is a red, tender lump that occurs when a hair follicle becomes infected, or infection enters a break in the skin from the outside. It comes to a head and bursts, or sometimes subsides without bursting. Boils are most common on the neck and buttocks. Infection can spread rapidly, causing more boils to develop, so avoid fingering a boil, and discourage your child from doing so.

WHAT TO LOOK OUT FOR

- Large, painful, red lump with a white centre
- A pussy head which bursts

HOW TO TREAT BOILS

- Wash with a salt solution and apply a clean dressing to prevent infection spreading.
- Don't squeeze the boil, as this will risk spreading it.
- Take your child to the doctor if the boil is unduly painful, if it shows signs of spreading, if it does not clear up within a week, or if you notice red streaks radiating from it.
- The doctor may lance the boil or prescribe antibiotics or a cream.
- Frequent outbreaks of boils are very occasionally a sign of diabetes. Consult the doctor.

BREATH HOLDING

Most children who have breath-holding attacks do so in the course of a temper tantrum or following a shock such as a fall. Your child may even become momentarily unconscious, but if this happens the automatic breathing mechanisms take over and she recovers. Unlike breathing problems caused by obstruction, breath holding is not life threatening, and children grow out of it.

WHAT TO LOOK OUT FOR

- Pale face
- Long screaming or crying fit followed by failure to breathe
- Unconsciousness
- Fits

HOW TO TREAT BREATH-HOLDING ATTACKS

- Remain calm and ignore it as much as you can. This may be difficult but if your child realizes she can use breath holding to gain your attention, she may take longer to grow out of it.
- If your child passes out leave her to recover naturally.
- Seek help from the doctor if breath holding becomes a habit.
- If your child does not start breathing as soon as she loses consciousness, give mouth-to-mouth resuscitation and get someone to summon medical help.

BRONCHIOLITIS

Bronchiolitis affects babies under one year old and is caused by a virus called respiratory syncytial virus (RSV). What usually happens is that a cough, cold, or other respiratory infection spreads, inflaming the small airways (bronchioles) in the lungs. These become swollen and blocked with mucus, causing the baby to fight for breath.

WHAT TO LOOK OUT FOR

- Unusually rapid breathing
- Fighting for breath
- Wheezing
- Raised temperature
- A bluish tinge to lips, tongue, nails

- Restlessness and irritability
- Drowsiness
- Dry cough

HOW TO TREAT BRONCHIOLITIS

- Call the doctor at once if your baby is having trouble breathing or if a cold or cough becomes suddenly much worse. Alternatively, call an ambulance or take your child straight to casualty.
- Try to remain calm yourself. If your baby senses your distress and starts to cry frantically it will be even more difficult for him to breathe.
- Give your baby small, frequent feeds if he is breast-fed. If he is bottle-fed, keep up his fluid intake.
- Bronchiolitis usually clears up within one to two weeks and may be treated at home, but in serious cases the doctor may want to admit your baby to hospital for observation.
- In more serious cases your baby may need oxygen treatment in hospital, or very occasionally to have his breathing taken over by a ventilator. A drug may be given to assist breathing. Although this can be very worrying, most babies make a complete recovery.
- Try to keep a young baby away from people with coughs, colds and virus infections.
- Keep your baby's bedroom a steady temperature and don't let it become too cold.

BRONCHITIS

Bronchitis is an inflammation of the larger air passages (bronchi) of the lung. It can be serious in babies. Acute bronchitis is not to be confused with the chronic type that affects older people. A minor respiratory infection, such as a cough or cold, invades the lungs, causing inflammation, swelling and the accumulation of mucus, which makes breathing difficult. The irritation causes a cough, and often vomiting.

WHAT TO LOOK OUT FOR

- Rapid, wheezy breathing

- Dry cough which later becomes bubbly
- Green or yellow sputum
- Headache, lethargy, lack of appetite
- Raised temperature
- Vomiting
- Bluish tinge to lips or tongue

HOW TO TREAT BRONCHITIS

- Keep your child warm and quiet. Exertion and overexcitement may make the condition worse. Make up a bed on the sofa if she does not want to stay in bed.
- Bring down your child's temperature with paracetamol syrup.
- Encourage her to cough up sputum by holding her, head down, across your knee or the arm of a chair or sofa during an attack of coughing.
- If her face turns bluish, especially around the lips, if her breathing becomes excessively laboured, or if any other symptoms become pronounced, call the doctor or take your child to casualty.
- Your child may be admitted to hospital for oxygen treatment.
- If your child's cough is keeping her awake at night the doctor may prescribe a soothing linctus. Do not attempt to suppress the cough with over-the-counter remedies.
- Protect your child from exposure to others' coughs and colds. If anyone in your household is a smoker your child stands a greater chance of developing bronchitis – a good reason to make a real effort to give up.
- A warm, humid atmosphere will help ease the condition.
- Keep an eye on the sputum your child produces. It should go from clear to green/yellow to clear again. Persistent yellow, green or brown phlegm may be a sign of infection which needs treating with antibiotics.

See also: Bronchiolitis; Colds; Cough; Pneumonia.

CHICKEN POX

This is normally a mild illness caused by the virus *varicella zoster*. It is spread by breathing in droplets breathed out by an infected person, and the incubation period is two to three weeks. A child is infectious from two to four days before the first spots develop until they have all developed scabs. The virus tends to occur in epidemics every two to three years. Once your child has had chicken pox he will be immune to the illness for the rest of his life. However, in later life exposure to the virus may cause shingles.

Your child will probably seem unwell for a day or so, then will develop crops of raised red spots first on the chest, abdomen and inner thighs, then on the face, scalp, arms and legs. The spots form blisters which are excruciatingly itchy before crusting over and dropping off. The spots come out in batches over the course of about four days and gradually disappear over the next couple of weeks.

Complications are rare, though occasionally pneumonia or even inflammation of the brain (encephalitis) occur if the virus attacks the lungs or brain.

The main problem is the discomfort of the spots, especially in delicate places like the mouth, anus or vagina. If your child scratches the scabs, scars occur which can take many years to fade.

WHAT TO LOOK OUT FOR

- Your child seems unwell, with general symptoms such as headache, sore throat, slightly raised temperature
- Raised, red spots appear in crops, which then form blisters, burst and scab over
- Crops of spots occur, so that at any one time your child has spots in various stages of development

HOW TO TREAT CHICKEN POX

- Give your child frequent cool showers or baths with a good handful of bicarbonate of soda added to the water to sooth itching.
- Apply calamine lotion or cream to allay irritation.
- Keep the rash clean and dry.
- Let your child rinse his mouth with salt water if he has spots in it.
- Keep him away from babies and other children.
- Keep your child's nails short to avoid scratching, which can cause scars. It might help to put scratch mittens on a baby.
- Make sure your child drinks plenty of fluids and has enough rest. If

he has problems sleeping because of itching, give him paracetamol syrup, not aspirin.

- If necessary take steps to bring down a high temperature (see page 12).
- If your baby has spots in the nappy area, change his nappies more frequently and use a one-way nappy liner to keep him dry and comfortable.
- See your doctor to confirm diagnosis, and again if your child starts to recover then becomes unwell again.
- Consult the doctor at once if your child develops signs of a respiratory infection or a severe headache and vomiting.
- If the spots become inflamed the doctor may prescribe an antibiotic cream.
- NEVER give aspirin in any form to a child with chicken pox because of the danger of Reye's syndrome, severe vomiting, confusion and fits, which can be fatal.

See also: Encephalitis; Reye's syndrome.

CHILBLAINS

Chilblains occur when the skin is exposed to changes in temperature. In cold, damp conditions the skin of the extremities, which are especially sensitive to changes in temperature, becomes pale and numb as a result of blood vessels beneath the surface closing up in order to retain heat. When the child then goes into a warm room the blood vessels expand again, causing the skin to become red and itchy.

The commonest sites are the toes, fingers, ears, ankles and backs of legs. Chilblains are not usually serious, and clear up in two to three weeks.

WHAT TO LOOK OUT FOR

- Red, swollen, itchy toes, fingers, ankles
- Extremities that go pale and numb with cold
- Pain
- Feelings of heat

HOW TO TREAT CHILBLAINS

- Wrap your toddler up warmly before letting her go out in cold, damp weather.
- In very cold weather use double layers of socks and gloves, fur-lined boots, hoods, thick trousers. Thermal fabrics are especially suitable.
- Keep your child's nails short and try to discourage her from scratching the chilblains. They itch furiously, but scratching will just make them worse. The chemist will have creams to soothe itching.
- Don't bathe your child's feet in hot water or mustard solution.

COELIAC DISEASE

Coeliac disease is a hereditary illness which affects one in two thousand children. It is caused by an allergy to gluten – a protein found in many cereals – which prevents the intestine from absorbing essential nutrients. It usually makes its appearance when the child is weaned on to solids, though sometimes it remains undetected until the child is older. The first signs are that the child stops thriving when he goes on to solids, and his bowel motions become bulky, soft, pale and smelly. If the condition remains unrecognized it can slow down the child's growth and development and lay him open to other infections. Nutrient deficiencies are responsible for other symptoms such as anaemia, sore tongue and thinning of the bones. If the disease is correctly diagnosed and your child is put on a gluten-free diet he will be able to live a completely normal, healthy life.

WHAT TO LOOK OUT FOR

- Failure to gain weight between 6 and 18 months old (regular weighing at the clinic will enable you to keep track of weight gain)
- Irritability, whining, weakness
- Swollen abdomen, wasted limbs
- Bulky, soft, pale, frequent bowel motions with a foul smell

HOW TO TREAT COELIAC DISEASE

- See your doctor if your baby or toddler is not gaining weight, if he is losing weight, and if he displays any of the other symptoms listed.

- The doctor will test your child's blood and stools for their fat content if coeliac disease is suspected. If tests are positive the doctor will probably admit your child to hospital, where a small snip of the lining of the intestine can be taken and examined for other signs of the illness.
- The doctor will advise you on a gluten-free diet and will refer you to a specialist, who will probably put you in touch with a dietician to help you put the diet into practice.
- The doctor may prescribe vitamins to make up for any deficiencies your child may be suffering as a result of the disease.
- The doctor may advise other members of the family to be tested, as the disease runs in families.
- If your child is diagnosed as coeliac you must not give him bread, cakes, buns, and hidden sources of gluten such as dried or tinned soups, chocolate powder, sausages, gravy powder or granules and so on. One of the excellent gluten-free recipe books that are available will help.
- It will be more convenient and make your child feel less the odd one out if you put the whole family on a gluten-free diet.
- Read labels on packaged food, so you can avoid hidden gluten in processed foods.

For advice and support contact: The Coeliac Society, P.O. Box 220, High Wycombe, Bucks HP11 2HY. Tel: 0494 37278.

COLDS

A cold is an infection of the air passages in the nose. There are literally hundreds of cold viruses, and so far no one has come up with a cure for any of them. Children tend to catch more colds than adults because they come into contact with them more often and have not yet built up any immunity. The average child catches six to eight colds a year. Colds are miserable, but they are not usually serious unless the virus passes on to the lungs and causes complications. The best you can do for a toddler or older child is to help ease the symptoms and wait for the cold to get better. In the case of a baby a cold can be more serious, as a blocked nose can interfere with feeding so your baby is deprived of the comfort she would normally get from sucking at the breast, bottle or a dummy. Moreover, by lowering the body's resistance a cold can also pave the way for other (secondary) infections, such as bronchitis and pneumonia.

WHAT TO LOOK OUT FOR

- Runny nose
- Sneezing
- Cough
- Red, watery eyes
- Croaky voice
- Raised temperature
- Listlessness and loss of appetite

HOW TO TREAT A COLD

- Give your child plenty of fluids.
- Raise the upper end of your child's bed or cot by putting books or bricks under the legs. Alternatively, put a pillow or rolled towel *under* the head end of the mattress.
- Provide a warm, moist atmosphere by boiling a kettle in the room, or taking your child into the bathroom and running the shower to generate steam, or even buying a special vaporizer to humidify the air.
- Antibiotics cannot cure a cold, as it is caused by a virus.
- Camphorated types of capsules squeezed on your child's pillow or clothing will help clear her nose and will aid breathing.
- Give your child hot lemon drinks to soothe a sore throat and help ease breathing through the nasal passages.
- *Don't* dose your child with proprietary cold cures or cough suppressants unless prescribed by the doctor. The cough is the body's way of dealing with excess mucus and prevents germs passing further down the air passages. Decongestants can be useful, however, taken as syrup or drops. Don't use nasal drops for longer than prescribed or instructed on the packet. Over-use can damage the delicate mucus membrane.
- Give your child paracetamol syrup to help her sleep at night.
- Teach a toddler how to blow her nose by blocking off one nostril at a time and blowing into a tissue.

- To prevent spreading germs, burn used tissues or put them in a plastic bag, seal and put in the dustbin.
- Keep your child away from other children and from friends or relations with babies.
- Treat a raised temperature (see page 12)
- Continuing cold symptoms may be caused by an allergy rather than a virus.

SEE THE DOCTOR IF:

- A baby less than six months old has a cold.
- Your baby or child develops other symptoms, such as earache, pain or swelling around the eyes or in the chest, a headache or an excessively sore throat.
- Your child's cough gets markedly worse and breathing difficulties develop.
- The discharge from your child's nose becomes yellow or greenish. This could indicate secondary infection and your child may need antibiotics.
- Your child coughs up green, yellow or grey sputum.
- The cold does not appear to be getting better after about four days. The worst of the cold should be over within four days, though it can take up to 10 days for all symptoms to disappear.
- Your child seems to be getting worse instead of better.

See also: Allergies; Bronchiolitis; Bronchitis; Cough; Croup; Earache; Hay fever; Headache; Laryngitis; Pneumonia; Sinusitis.

COLD SORES

These are caused by the *herpes simplex* virus, which attacks the nerve cells. Many people carry the virus but not all develop symptoms. Sometimes a person may have just one or two attacks and then never have any more. A first attack of the virus may occur between the ages of six months and five years, in which case the child sometimes develops blisters, sores and mouth ulcers, which make eating difficult and painful.

After a first attack the virus is thought to lie dormant in the nerve cells until something triggers off an attack of cold sores. Common triggers are a rise in temperature following an infection or sunbathing, exposure to extremes of cold or heat, stress, and lowered resistance due to other illnesses. The first sign is an itchy, tingling sensation around the mouth and face, followed by one or several blisters which scab over within three to five days before dropping off. Complete healing occurs within about two weeks.

As cold sores are caused by a virus there is no cure for them, but there is much you can do to make your child more comfortable. If he seems especially susceptible to cold sores the doctor can prescribe an anti-viral medicine to try and ward off subsequent attacks.

WHAT TO LOOK OUT FOR

- A crop of mouth ulcers
- An itchy, tingling feeling, followed by reddened spots around the lips and face
- Blisters that scab over and fall off

HOW TO TREAT COLD SORES

- Give your child paracetamol syrup to allay pain and discomfort.
- If your child has mouth ulcers let him sip iced water, and if he is a toddler teach him how to rinse out his mouth with an over-the-counter mouthwash. Give him soft, cool foods to eat. Let him drink through a straw to bypass ulcers.
- Apply cool compresses to alleviate itching and soreness.
- Make sure your child is scrupulous over hand washing and other hygiene practices.
- Each member of the family should have his or her own towel and flannel.
- Try to discourage your toddler from fingering a cold sore, and discourage him from direct contact, such as kissing, with other children while he has open sores.
- If the cold sore becomes infected or pussy, or if your child gets cold sores when he has eczema, take him to see the doctor.
- Report to the doctor if your child gets cold sores near his eyes.
- The doctor may prescribe an antibiotic cream to deal with secondary infection, and/or an anti-viral ointment (Acyclovir) to try and ward off future attacks.

COLIC

This may occur about two to three weeks after birth, and lasts for between three and six months. The baby cries and draws up her legs as though in pain. Bursts of inconsolable crying occur, often at a regular time each day. Despite her apparent distress during an attack, your baby should be well and thriving at other times.

No one really knows what causes colic. It has been attributed to various factors – such as cow's milk allergy, an immature digestive system, or stress – but nothing has been proved. There is no real cure for colic, though in severe cases the doctor may prescribe an anti-colic medicine or sedative.

WHAT TO LOOK OUT FOR

- Prolonged bursts of crying, often at the same time each day, usually lasting for more than three hours a day and going on for more than three weeks
- Your baby draws up her legs and clenches her fists as though in pain
- Your baby may gnaw her fists and behave as though she is hungry. However, sucking brings only temporary comfort.

HOW TO TREAT COLIC

- See the doctor to confirm diagnosis. Occasionally a prescribed anti-colic remedy can help – ask your health visitor or doctor.
- If your baby is bottle-fed check her bottle, making sure that the hole in the teat is not too large or too small.
- Wind your baby carefully. Colic can be aggravated by wind, and if your child is already in discomfort wind may make her feel even worse.
- If you are breast-feeding try cutting dairy food out of your diet for a couple of weeks and see if there is any improvement. Beware of hidden dairy foods in products such as margarine, packet soups and so on. Do make sure you take in enough calcium from other foods.
- Don't dose your baby with over-the-counter medicines or gripe water, as they rarely help.
- Trial and error will help you discover what soothes your baby most

effectively. Sucking – from bottle, breast, dummy or your finger – may quieten her for a while.

- Try rhythmic rocking or movement. A walk in the pram, a drive around the block in the car, or strapping your child to you in a baby carrier as you go about your daily life, may help soothe her to sleep. You can also try draping her facing downwards over your forearm and rhythmically rocking her. This so-called 'colic hold' sometimes works wonders.
- Gentle warmth against your baby's stomach may help. Try resting her on your lap over a well-swaddled hot-water bottle, or warm her crib with a hot-water bottle before placing her in it stomach down.
- Noise – singing, music, taped womb noises, or household sounds such as a vacuum cleaner, washing machine or tumble drier – sometimes helps.
- Try putting your baby on a lambskin in her cot.
- A warm bath may be soothing and helps pass the time.
- If your baby has diarrhoea, blood in her motions, a high temperature (over 37.8°C/100°F), or other signs of illness, call the doctor.

Tips for parents of a baby with colic

Colic is extremely wearing for parents, so you need to look after yourself too.
- Don't feel guilty if your baby has colic; it is not your fault.
- Don't believe anyone who tells you your baby has colic because she is picking up your anxiety. A screaming baby whom you can do little to comfort is enough to make the most well-balanced person anxious.
- Try to get help with your chores. If you are able to enjoy some rest and relaxation you will be better able to cope with the crying.
- Take some time off for yourself. Don't use it to catch up on the ironing; use it as time for you.
- Do bear in mind that however awful it seems at the time, colic does get better in the end.

For advice and support contact: Crysis, BCM Cry-sis, London WC1N 3XX.

See also: Intussusception.

CONJUNCTIVITIS

Conjunctivitis is inflammation of the membrane that covers the eyeball and the inside of the eyelid. It can be caused by a virus or bacteria or by getting a speck of dust or grit in the eye. It can also be a sign of allergy or, in the case of a baby, a blocked tear duct. Your child will have red, itchy, watery eyes and may dislike bright light. When he wakes in the morning his eyelids and lashes are gummed up with pus. Conjunctivitis is highly contagious, so make sure your child has his own separate towel and flannel.

WHAT TO LOOK OUT FOR

- Red, sore eyes
- Sticky eyes, with matted lashes in the morning
- Dislike of bright light
- Itchy, gritty sensation
- Swollen eyelids

HOW TO TREAT CONJUNCTIVITIS

- Swab your child's eyes with cotton wool dipped in warm, boiled water, using a separate swab for each eye. Swab from the corners of the eyelid nearest the nose outwards.
- If your child is old enough you can use an eyebath containing either an over-the-counter eye solution or a solution of 5 ml of salt to one glass of warm water.
- Be especially careful about hygiene; keep your own hands scrupulously clean and encourage your child to do likewise. Make sure your child has a separate towel and flannel, otherwise the infection may spread.
- If your baby is suffering from conjunctivitis take him to the doctor, who may want to prescribe an antibiotic ointment or drops.
- If the problem persists your baby may need a simple probing operation to clear the duct towards the end of his first year.
- If a newborn baby has an eye infection you should treat it more seriously. Report it to the doctor immediately so that treatment can be started without delay.

How to apply eye drops

1. Wrap your baby in a shawl or blanket, and get someone else to hold him if possible. Hold his upper lid open and aim the drops into the corner of his eye closest to his nose.
2. Sit your toddler in a chair and tilt his head back in order to apply the drops.
3. If using ointment, gently pull down your child's lower lid and smear some ointment along it, working from the side nearest his nose to the outer lid.
4. Always throw away any eye ointment or drops that are left over, as they could be contaminated.

CONSTIPATION

Constipation refers to dry, hard bowel motions that are difficult to pass. It does not refer to the number of bowel motions your child has, nor their regularity. For instance, some children open their bowels only once every few days. So long as the motion is soft, this is the normal pattern for that child and not a cause for concern.

Breast-fed babies are normally never constipated. It is quite normal for a breast-fed baby to dirty her nappy only after several days, or even a week. Though the amount may be copious, the texture of the stools is soft. Bottle-fed babies are more prone to constipation. Ask your health visitor for advice on how to cope with this. It is usually simply a matter of giving your baby extra feeds.

Some babies make a great performance of opening their bowels! They go bright red in the face, clench their fists and grunt and strain. Only rarely is this caused by constipation. If the stool is soft in consistency then your child is not constipated.

Constipation may become a problem when your baby is weaned. A faddy toddler, who is not eating a balanced diet because she rejects roughage in the form of fruit or vegetables, or who is not getting sufficient drinks, may have a tendency to become constipated. The remedy is simply to include more high-fibre foods in her diet.

If you become embroiled in a battle of wills over toilet training, your toddler may hold back her bowel motions in an attempt to defy you. In this case constipation is often a side effect, and the solution is to relax potty training for a while to allow your child to return to normal. Better still, to avoid the problem arising try to be calm about the whole business from the start.

The only other time a baby or toddler may experience constipation is during a feverish illness, when the body absorbs liquid from your child's stools in an attempt to prevent dehydration. Your child's bowels will return to normal once the illness is over.

At one time parents used to be very concerned about the state of their children's bowels, and it was believed that a daily bowel motion was necessary for good health. We now know this is an old-fashioned attitude, but you may find your parents or grandparents are worried by your baby or toddler's toilet habits. Try to ignore their well-meant advice, and don't let them persuade you to put pressure on your child.

HOW TO TREAT CONSTIPATION

- Make sure your toddler eats plenty of fruit and vegetables and drinks enough fluids. If she is reluctant to drink from a cup, she may be more inclined to drink from a feeder cup, her bottle, or a fancy cup.
- If your child does become constipated, a bowl of stewed prunes, apricots, or reconstituted dried fruit salad will usually solve the problem.
- Don't be tempted to give your child laxatives or suppositories unless advised to do so by your doctor.
- Don't leave your toddler for hours on her potty. If she is afraid of the 'big' toilet, let her use a potty, or place a couple of blocks on either side of the toilet for her to rest her feet on. Many toddlers feel insecure if lifted on to the toilet and left with their legs dangling.
- Ignore pressures from members of the older generation to toilet train your youngster or to watch her bowels. Don't transmit any anxiety you may feel about the whole business to your child.
- If your baby or toddler complains of pain on passing a motion, has blood in her motions or is frequently constipated, see the doctor. If she has developed a small tear in the anus (anal fissure) through straining to pass a difficult motion she may be reluctant to open her bowels. The doctor will prescribe a special soothing cream and perhaps a stool-softening suppository for use until the problem has cleared up.

See also: Abdominal pain; Anal fissure; Appendicitis.

CONVULSION

Convulsion is simply the medical term for a fit. The most common cause of fits in babies or toddlers is having a feverish illness which 'irritates' their immature brain. The child loses consciousness, his body goes stiff, his arms and legs twitch, and he may foam at the mouth or lose control of his bowels and bladder. The fit generally lasts a matter of seconds or minutes, and afterwards he will be disorientated and exhausted. Such fits, which are called febrile convulsions, are generally harmless, though they are extremely alarming to watch. If your child has had one febrile convulsion, especially if he was under one year old, there is a fair chance he might have another one the next time he runs a high temperature. This is useful to know so you can be vigilant and take steps to bring his temperature down if he does become feverish. Febrile convulsions tend to run in families, and one in 25 children under the age of five has them.

Very occasionally such a fit can be a sign of epilepsy, especially if the convulsion is a long one (more than 15 minutes), if there are signs that it is affecting one particular part of the brain, or if the illness runs in the family. Diabetes, meningitis and encephalitis are other rare, more serious causes of convulsions.

WHAT TO LOOK OUT FOR

- A sudden rise in temperature
- Loss of consciousness
- Stiffness
- Jerking muscles
- Lack of bowel and bladder control
- A bluish tinge to the face or lips
- Confusion and drowsiness on recovery

HOW TO TREAT A CONVULSION

- To prevent your child from hurting himself remove all dangerous objects. Don't attempt to restrain him. You can lie a baby over your knee head downwards, to ensure his breathing passages remain open.
- Never leave a child who is having a convulsion alone. Loosen his clothing to make sure he can breathe.

- Once the fit is over, turn him on to his side to ensure that his air passages are free.
- Don't attempt to give him any medicine or drinks.
- Contact the doctor, who may want to admit your child to hospital for special tests to rule out any serious causes of the convulsion.
- Stay calm.
- Take your child straight to hospital if the convulsion lasts longer than 10–15 minutes.
- Follow the steps on page 12 to bring your child's temperature down.

See also: Diabetes; Encephalitis; Epilepsy; Meningitis.

COUGH

A cough is not an illness as such but a symptom of some other ailment such as a chest infection, cold, sinus infection, asthma or other allergy, whooping cough or tonsillitis. Children who are regularly exposed to other people's cigarette smoke (passive smoking) are also more liable to suffer from coughs and other respiratory problems. The cough is caused by irritation of the air passages, either by phlegm or by a foreign body. Your child coughs to get rid of the cause of the irritation, which is why you should never suppress your child's cough except on the advice of your doctor. The cough is a protective mechanism which can prevent infection going further down the air passages to the lungs. A wet, bubbly cough may be an indication that the cough has reached your child's lungs and needs medical treatment. Of course, if your child goes blue in the face with a cough, or seems to be having undue difficulty breathing, you should also contact the doctor.

WHAT TO LOOK OUT FOR

- Whether the cough is dry or bubbly
- Whether the cough is worse at certain times.

SEE THE DOCTOR IF:

- She has a persistent cough and is aged less than three months.
- She is wheezing, or is having difficulty breathing.

- She is running a high temperature.
- The cough is caused by her swallowing a foreign body.
- The cough does not improve within three to four days.
- She has a hacking cough.
- She appears to have earache.
- The cough is spasmodic and your child vomits after a fit of coughing – in this case the cough could be a sign of whooping cough.
- She suffers any other chronic illness.

HOW TO TREAT A COUGH

- Treatment depends on the cause. If the doctor suspects that the cough is a result of a bacterial infection he or she may prescribe antibiotics.
- Don't give medicine to suppress the cough unless your doctor advises it. Help make your baby or child more comfortable by propping a child up at night with several pillows or raising the head of a baby's cot by placing a pillow under the mattress. Patting her on the back during a coughing fit will help loosen any phlegm and enable her to cough it up.
- If your child has swallowed something use your finger to try and hook it out or follow the suggestions on page 37.
- Keep your child quiet and warm, and don't let her run around too much as this may make her more liable to cough.
- Don't smoke in the rooms your child uses. Give her plenty of drinks, especially hot ones such as honey and lemon. A steamy atmosphere will help clear her air passages.

See also: Allergies; Asthma; Bronchiolitis; Bronchitis; Colds; Croup; Influenza; Laryngitis; Whooping cough.

CRADLE CAP

Cradle cap is a thick, yellowish, scaly coating covering the scalp. It is most common in babies, though children up to three can suffer from it too. Although it is usually confined to the scalp it can spread to other parts such as the forehead or eyebrows, or warm, moist areas such as the groin. Cradle cap is unsightly but not harmful. Don't worry that your baby's condition is a result of lack of hygiene; it is just that some babies have greasier scalps than others. Cradle cap is easily treatable at home, though it often recurs in which case it will need further treatment.

WHAT TO LOOK OUT FOR

- Thick, creamy-yellow greasy scales on the scalp

HOW TO TREAT CRADLE CAP

- Wash your baby's scalp thoroughly every day, rubbing it gently. Don't be afraid you will damage his head when you wash him. Although the soft bones of his skull are not yet fully fused, they are protected by a thick membrane over the gaps (the fontanelles).
- Brush your baby's hair every day, even if he only has a little, to prevent the build-up of scales.
- Loosen the scales by applying a little baby oil or olive oil to your baby's scalp before he goes to bed. The next morning they should be easy to comb or shampoo off. Alternatively use a proprietary preparation from the chemist.
- If the condition does not respond to home treatment or if the skin seems red, scaly or inflamed elsewhere, consult the doctor as your baby may have a type of eczema.
- Don't use an anti-dandruff shampoo unless your doctor advises it.

See also: Eczema.

CROUP

Croup is the term used for a particular sort of dry, barking cough. It is caused by the inflammation and constriction of the windpipe – usually as a result of a cold or other infection, such as bronchitis. The characteristic croupy bark is caused as the air is expelled past the voice box. It most often occurs in children under three, because their tiny air passages, or bronchi, constrict. Attacks occur without warning – often after your child has developed a cold and usually at night – and can be very alarming as your child fights for breath.

Occasionally croup can occur if your child has inhaled a small object, such as a bead. A child with serious croup who is finding it difficult to breathe needs urgent medical attention. Fortunately repeated attacks are rare, but some children do suffer from more attacks than others and this could be linked to some kind of allergic reaction.

WHAT TO LOOK OUT FOR

- A dry, barking cough, rather like the sound made by a sea lion
- Difficulty breathing in – your child's lower chest may sink every time she draws in her breath
- Wheezing
- High temperature
- In severe cases a greyish or blue tinge to the complexion

HOW TO TREAT CROUP

- Don't leave your child alone while she is suffering an attack.
- Breathing in warm, moist air should bring immediate relief. Take your child into the bathroom and run the hot tap or shower to fill the room with steam. Alternatively boil a kettle in your child's room – but take care she does not go too near or she may scald herself.
- Stay calm – if your child senses you are worried she will find breathing even more difficult.
- Keep your child upright, as it is easier for her to breathe if she is vertical. Sit her propped up with pillows.
- If the attack occurs on a cool, damp night, open the window and let your child breathe the cool night air.
- If the attack does not ease progressively within an hour or so, or if it gets worse, call the doctor.
- If your child is ill, if she has a temperature of more than 39°C (102.2°F), if her croup is so bad that she has difficulty breathing, or if she turns blue, call the doctor or take your child to the nearest hospital casualty department, as she may need artificial help.
- Don't give your child cough syrups.
- If your child does suffer repeated attacks the doctor may advise that you buy a special vaporizer to keep the air in her room moist.

See also: Asthma; Bronchitis; Cough; Laryngitis; Whooping cough.

DEAFNESS

One in 1,000 children is either partially or completely deaf. Deafness
may be a result of lack of oxygen during birth, premature birth, or some
developmental abnormality caused by German measles or occasionally
by another, rare infection. Sometimes deafness is hereditary. If there is
a history of it in your family a genetic counsellor will be able to advise
you on the likelihood of your baby inheriting it. Deafness can also
occur in children as a result of an ear infection (see Glue ear and Otitis
media), certain acute virus infections, or physical injury to the ear.
Complete deafness in both ears is extremely rare in children.
    It is hard to detect deafness in a newborn baby. All babies 'screen
out' sounds that do not interest them, and it may not be until your baby
seems slow to respond to sounds, or to talk, that you suspect he is not
hearing as he should. Most babies 'coo' and 'babble' long before they
can actually say anything, and a failure to do this can sometimes be a
warning of hearing problems. If you suspect your child is not hearing
properly, have a word with your GP or health visitor, who will be able
to arrange for special tests to be carried out if necessary. Some hospitals
have a special machine called an Auditory Response Cradle (ARC),
which tests how well a newborn baby responds to sound. If hearing loss
is suspected, further tests can be carried out.

WHAT TO LOOK OUT FOR

- Not startled by loud noises
- Does not 'talk' to you
- Slow in learning to talk properly

HOW TO TREAT DEAFNESS

- Consult your doctor or health visitor if you suspect your baby or
  child is having difficulties with hearing, or if he seems to be suffering
  from lack of hearing following an ear infection.
- A baby can be fitted with a hearing aid from six months of age.
- Decongestants might help if your child suffers from catarrh.
- If your child becomes deaf as a result of repeated ear infections he
  may need simple surgery to drain fluid from his ears.
- If your child is deaf, always look directly at him when you speak to

him, so he can learn to lip-read and associate the sounds you make with your movements.
- Speak slowly and clearly, and make sure that other people do so too.
- If your child is diagnosed as deaf you can get support and help from other parents of deaf children. There may be special playgroups for deaf children in your area.

For advice and support contact: The National Deaf Children's Society, 45 Hereford Road, London W2 5AH. Tel: 01-229 9272/4. It offers useful advice, booklets and so on.

See also: Glue ear; Otitis media; Wax in the ears.

DEHYDRATION

Seventy per cent of the body is made up of water. If this water becomes depleted, as a result of vomiting, diarrhoea or fever, the body has insufficient fluid to carry minerals and to maintain its chemical balance. When this occurs the volume of blood circulating can reach dangerously low levels and become too concentrated. Dehydration is extremely serious and if left untreated can lead to brain damage and even death. This is why diarrhoea lasting more than six hours should always be taken seriously in a baby or small child.

WHAT TO LOOK OUT FOR
- Dry mouth and skin, especially around the tongue and lips
- Drowsiness and lack of energy
- Dry nappies or little urine when your child passes water
- Sunken eyes or fontanelles (soft spots) in a baby
- Raised temperature

HOW TO TREAT DEHYDRATION
- If your child has a temperature try to bring it down using the measures outlined on page 12.
- If your baby is breast-fed give her frequent feeds. If she is bottle-fed, stop giving milk and give her cool, boiled water from a spoon, bottle or dropper. If your baby has not stopped vomiting or having

diarrhoea after six hours consult the doctor. Your baby may need a special rehydrating solution to rebalance her body chemicals.

- Give your child small, frequent drinks of water or diluted fruit juice – not milk or concentrated fruit juice. Aim for 50 ml (2 fl oz) per hour for a baby; and 100 ml (4 fl oz) per hour for a pre-school child.
- If dehydration is severe your child may need to be admitted to hospital, where a special drip can be set up to replace lost fluid and minerals.
- Keep a special rehydrating mixture (available from the chemist) in stock. Don't give other over-the-counter remedies for diarrhoea and vomiting unless advised to by your doctor.
- As your child recovers, gradually reintroduce her milk feeds. The health visitor will advise you on how to do this.

See also: Diarrhoea; Fever; Gastroenteritis; Vomiting.

DIABETES

Each year over 1,500 children in the UK develop diabetes – the condition in which there is too much sugar in the blood. It is very rare in newborn babies and toddlers. Diabetes occurs following the failure of the pancreas to manufacture the hormone insulin. Insulin is responsible for breaking down sugar in the body, which is produced after eating carbohydrates. Once broken down, this sugar is either used as energy, for repairing body tissues, or is stored in the liver. If the body is short of insulin the level of sugar in the blood rises and the body is deprived of energy. In order to compensate, the body starts to break down fats and proteins, which results in weight loss and the release of poisonous wastes such as ketones. Weight loss, thirst, frequent passing of large amounts of urine, lack of energy, and irritability are all early signs of diabetes, which has a tendency to run in some families. There is no cure for it, but it can be kept under control with careful diet and injections of insulin.

WHAT TO LOOK OUT FOR

- Excessive thirst
- Passing large amounts of urine, which may smell sweet
- Weight loss

- Tiredness, irritability, lack of energy
- Frequent minor infections
- Smell of acetone (pear drops) on the breath

HOW TO TREAT DIABETES

- Once diabetes is confirmed treatment is aimed at keeping your child's body in balance by means of insulin injections and diet. It can be quite difficult to stick a needle in your own child. But after the first few occasions your child will grow to accept it as a normal part of his life.
- The hospital will give you special equipment to use at home in order to test your child's urine. Alternatively it is possible to buy a battery-operated blood-sugar-test meter, which monitors insulin levels more accurately.
- The district nurse or health visitor will be a great support to you, and can help in the early days while you become accustomed to giving injections. Share the task of giving injections with your child's father.
- When giving your child an injection, direct the needle in at right angles. A plastic syringe, which you can get on prescription, is the best sort to use. There is no need to use spirit on your child's skin. If your baby has diabetes aim to give the injection 30 minutes before a feed.
- Diabetic babies under four months old need to have a night feed to keep their bodies in balance. Ask your doctor or health visitor for advice about breast- or bottle-feeding.
- Once your baby is weaned, be flexible. If he refuses solids you may be able to replace carbohydrates with fluids. Natural toddler faddiness is more difficult to cope with because it can disturb the blood sugar balance – the answer is to substitute foods from the same food group for the ones your child dislikes. Your health visitor will advise on this.
- It is a good idea for your child to wear a medic-alert bracelet in case he has any problems when you are not with him. Remember to tell other adults about his condition, such as playgroup leaders, babysitters, and anyone you leave him with.
- Take your child regularly to the hospital diabetic clinic where his growth will be carefully monitored.

- Try not to make your child feel different because of his condition.

For advice and support contact. The British Diabetic Association, 10 Queen Anne Street, London W1M 0BD. Tel: 01-323 1531.

DIARRHOEA

Diarrhoea refers to frequent loose, watery bowel motions. It happens when the intestines become inflamed, causing food to progress through them faster than normally. Consequently the body does not absorb enough water from the food and this can result in dehydration. Causes of diarrhoea include food poisoning, food intolerance (often of milk), a change of diet, and viruses. It can also be a symptom of some other infection elsewhere in the body, such as flu, an ear infection, a cough or a cold.

WHAT TO LOOK OUT FOR

- Watery, loose bowel motions that occur frequently
- Abdominal pain
- Possibly raised temperature

HOW TO TREAT DIARRHOEA

- Check for signs of dehydration (see page 84).
- See the doctor if your child is under one year old and has had diarrhoea for over six hours, or if the diarrhoea is accompanied by vomiting.
- Treat raised temperature as described on page 12.
- Rest your child's digestive system by withholding food and milk. Instead give frequent drinks of diluted fruit juice, plain water, or rehydrating mix from the chemist. After a day, gradually reintroduce food, keeping it plain and light.
- The doctor may prescribe a special rehydrating fluid and advise bed rest.
- If your baby is very ill she may need to be admitted to hospital, where she will have a drip set up to maintain the balance of fluid and chemicals in her body.

- When preparing your baby's food be scrupulously hygienic at all times.
- Keep your baby away from anyone suffering from diarrhoea.
- Occasionally, loose stools can be a sign of a more serious illness. See the doctor if your child's bowel motions are greasy and unpleasant smelling, or if there is any blood or mucus in his stools.

See also: Dehydration; Food poisoning; Gastroenteritis; Influenza; Otitis media; Vomiting.

DIPHTHERIA

Since the introduction of immunization, diphtheria, once one of the great childhood killer diseases, has all but died out. Nonetheless, epidemics do occasionally occur. It is a bacterial infection, the symptoms of which are similar to tonsillitis. The infection causes the release of toxins which attack and destroy healthy tissue. If left untreated it can lead to pneumonia and heart failure. The incubation period is between one to seven days and the illness lasts between one and three weeks. Healthy people may be carriers without having the infection themselves. The best protection you can offer your child is to have him immunized against the disease. Diphtheria is always serious, so if you suspect your child has it you should contact the doctor at once.

WHAT TO LOOK OUT FOR

- Slightly raised temperature
- Sore throat
- Cough that sounds like croup
- Headache
- Swollen tonsils covered by a greyish film

HOW TO TREAT DIPHTHERIA

- Protect your child from diphtheria by making sure he is up to date with his immunizations. You will usually be aware if there is an outbreak of the disease in your area.
- Check your child's tonsils for signs of the characteristic grey film. If

you suspect diphtheria call the doctor immediately. Your child will be admitted to hospital.

- The doctor will take a throat swab and prescribe antibiotics and antitoxins to prevent tissue damage. If your child is having breathing difficulties a tracheotomy – an operation to insert a tube into the windpipe – may be carried out to keep his breathing passages clear.

See also: Sore throat; Tonsillitis.

DIZZINESS

A feeling of lack of balance and unsteadiness, dizziness may occur if your child has an ear or throat infection. It can also be a symptom of anaemia, head injury, or – very rarely – a brain tumour. Dizziness sometimes happens in the prelude to a fit (convulsion). Short dizzy spells are not usually serious, but if your child feels dizzy for longer than 12 hours, if the dizziness is associated with vomiting or loss of co-ordination, or if she loses consciousness take her to a doctor.

WHAT TO LOOK OUT FOR

- Unsteadiness, particularly after exertion
- Loss of co-ordination
- Vomiting
- Loss of consciousness

HOW TO TREAT DIZZINESS

- Sit your child down quietly for a while.
- Put her head between her knees and encourage her to breathe deeply – this should alleviate most dizziness.
- Note any other symptoms. Usually dizziness is a symptom of some other condition and will get better when that is treated.

See also: Anaemia; Convulsion; Earache.

EARACHE

Earache is a common symptom in babies and young children. It is

usually a sign of middle ear infection (otitis media), which is often
caused when germs from the throat enter the ear. Earache can also be
caused by toothache, tonsillitis, mumps (because of swollen glands), or
infection of the outer ear (otitis externa). General congestion from a
cold can result in earache, as can going out in a cold wind without a hat
on. Changes in pressure, for example when travelling in an aeroplane,
can also produce earache; this usually passes off once the plane has
landed. Children are especially prone to ear infections because the tube
that joins the back of the nose, the throat and the ear (the Eustachian
tube) is only short. Hence germs from the nose and throat do not have
to spread very far before causing inflammation, pain and swelling.
Some children seem especially prone to middle ear infections.

WHAT TO LOOK OUT FOR

- A baby will not be able to tell you when he has earache, but he may
  pull or rub his ear and appear in discomfort
- Complaints of pain in or around the ear
- A blocked or runny nose
- A discharge of pus from the ear
- Swollen glands in the neck and elsewhere
- Tonsillitis
- Raised temperature
- Deafness, dizziness or headache
- Sleeplessness
- Vomiting

HOW TO TREAT EARACHE

- Consult your doctor if your child complains of earache, especially if he
  has a raised temperature or if there is a discharge of pus from his ear.
- Paracetamol syrup will relieve pain.
- Make sure your child takes any antibiotics prescribed.
- Never put anything down his ear.
- A warm pad of cotton wool, a heating pad or a hot-water bottle
  swaddled in a towel or clean nappy will help ease the pain.
- Do not let your child go swimming or get water in his ear during a
  bath.

See also: Otitis externa; Otitis media.

ECZEMA

More than two million people in this country suffer from eczema, and a large number of these are children. Eczema starts with a scaly, red, itchy patch of skin, which may eventually weep and crust over. It is not known what causes it, and in fact there are several different types. The most common type in children is *atopic* or allergic eczema, which tends to run in families. Children with this sort of eczema often go on to develop hay fever, asthma or other allergies later in life. The mechanism of food intolerance is not well understood, but cow's milk – either in formula milk, or in dairy foods eaten by a breast-fed baby's mother – is a common trigger. Other foods, such as eggs and wheat, can also be culprits, which is why many babies develop eczema when solids are first introduced to their diet. External irritants such as rough clothing, bacterial infection, washing powders, and stress can aggravate or bring on attacks. Dealing with a child who has eczema can be trying, and it is important to ensure you have plenty of support from those around you, as well as to take some time off from a crying, irritable, scratching child. There is no cure for eczema but it can be controlled very well using a combination of self-help methods and medical treatment. The good news is that as the immune system matures and becomes better able to deal with foreign substances, many children grow out of their eczema.

Another type of eczema, *seborrhoeic* eczema, occurs in areas rich in sebaceous glands, such as the outer ear (otitis externa), on the scalp (cradle cap), and on and around the eyelids and lashes, where it is known as blepharitis. In this type of eczema the irritation is much less troublesome.

ATOPIC ECZEMA – WHAT TO LOOK OUT FOR

- Dry, red, scaly skin, often starting on the face and head, and sometimes with patches on the forearms and lower legs
- Intense itchiness
- The eczema patches may weep and crust over
- Attacks may be made worse by outside factors such as cold, wind, stress and so on

HOW TO TREAT ATOPIC ECZEMA

- Keep the skin well-moisturized. Use a bland baby oil in the bath to prevent the skin drying out, and avoid soap and water. Apply a soothing, aqueous cream (available from the chemist) after washing.
- At the first sign of an attack apply an aqueous cream to soothe itching.
- Keep your child's fingernails short and put scratch mittens on a baby to prevent scratching.
- Avoid anything that irritates the skin and causes your child to scratch. Do not use wool next to the skin; cotton or cotton mixes are better. Wool-upholstered furniture and carpets can also be irritating.
- Make sure your child does not get sweaty as this causes itching. Avoid heavy layers of clothing, high household temperatures and over-activity.
- If patches of dry, itchy skin carry on for more than two or three weeks, if the itching is unbearable for your child, or if there is a family history of allergies such as asthma and eczema, consult your doctor. He or she may prescribe a mild steroid ointment to ease the condition. Use this carefully according to the doctor's instructions. The doctor may also prescribe a sedative to help your child sleep better.
- Try to pinpoint what triggers your child's eczema attacks. This means trying to identify particular foods or other substances that spark off the eczema. Your doctor, health visitor or dietician at the hospital will be able to help you. Alternatively contact the National Eczema Society (address below). Try not to be too disappointed if, despite your efforts, you cannot track down one particular factor.
- Try to maintain a calm, happy atmosphere – stress can make things worse. Remember that many children grow out of their eczema in time. And for those that don't, new research is coming up with some excellent anti-allergy drugs which are being improved all the time.

SEBORRHOEIC ECZEMA – WHAT TO LOOK OUT FOR

- Cradle cap
- Red, scaly patches around the ears, on the chest and back, and in other greasy areas such as the nose, ears and groin
- Little or no itching

HOW TO TREAT SEBORRHOEIC ECZEMA

- Follow the tips for atopic eczema and see specific entries for cradle cap and otitis externa.
- See the doctor if simple remedies do not clear up the eczema, or if there is a pussy discharge. Your doctor may prescribe a skin cream or lotion, or steroids.

For advice and support contact: The National Eczema Society, Tavistock House North, Tavistock Square, London WC1H 9SR. Tel: 01-388 4097.

See also: Allergies; Cradle cap; Otitis externa.

ENCEPHALITIS

Encephalitis, or inflammation of the brain, is an extremely rare complication of several otherwise harmless virus infections, such as mumps, measles, chicken pox or cold sores. It can also occur following bacterial infections or, on extremely rare occasions, following a vaccination for whooping cough. It develops suddenly, and your child will need immediate medical attention.

WHAT TO LOOK OUT FOR

- Headache
- Irritability and/or apathy
- Raised temperature
- Fits
- Intolerance of bright light
- Drowsiness and confusion
- Lack of appetite and/or vomiting

HOW TO TREAT ENCEPHALITIS

- Consult your doctor immediately if you suspect encephalitis. Your child will need to be admitted to hospital for special tests to confirm the diagnosis and treatment. Tests include a lumbar puncture, in which fluid is drawn from around the spinal cord and brain, and

various types of brain scan. Treatment includes the prescription of
anti-viral drugs, painkillers and anti-convulsant medication.
* Expect your child to take a while to recover, and to be more clingy
than usual. He may be left with some muscle weakness. Ask the
physiotherapist if there are any exercises you can do with him to
help strengthen his weakened muscles.

See also: Chicken pox; Cold sores; Convulsion; Measles; Meningitis;
Mumps; Whooping cough.

EPILEPSY

Epilepsy is a condition in which abnormal electrical impulses occur
within the brain, causing recurrent seizures. It can be brought on by
birth injury or as an after-effect of virus illnesses, but in many cases the
cause remains a mystery. It tends to run in families.

There are two different forms of epilepsy. The main type affecting
children under three is *grand mal*, which involves sudden loss of
consciousness and stiffening of the limbs, followed by rhythmic jerking
and shaking. After this the child becomes confused and drowsy and
usually falls asleep. These fits are indistinguishable from febrile
convulsions – the type of fit brought on by a high temperature. If your
child has a fit, do remember that the vast majority of fits affecting
children under five are of the harmless febrile type. If your child is
diagnosed as suffering from epilepsy she may need special attention
throughout her life. Fortunately epilepsy can be well controlled these
days using anti-convulsant drugs, and it should be possible for your
child to lead a normal life. There is no reason why, with a degree of
extra care, she should not enjoy sports and other childhood activities.
Epilepsy is not a mental illness. Sometimes a fit can be triggered off by a
specific factor such as flickering lights, a badly adjusted TV set, or
stress. You will come to recognize your child's particular triggers and
can help her to avoid them. As she grows older your child will learn to
recognize for herself the subtle signs that can indicate an imminent
attack.

The second type of epilepsy affecting children is *petit mal*. This does
not involve a fit. Instead the child looks 'blank', there is lip-smacking
and chewing, and she loses consciousness for a second or so. When she
comes to, she carries on as normal, unaware that anything untoward

has occurred. If your child suffers this form of epilepsy she may grow out of it at adolescence.

WHAT TO LOOK OUT FOR

Grand mal
- Loss of consciousness
- Stiffening of the limbs, clenching of the teeth
- Rhythmic twitching and shaking
- The child wets herself. She may also bite her tongue or froth at the mouth

Petit mal (children over three)
- Brief, trancelike state, after which the child recovers as if nothing has happened

HOW TO TREAT EPILEPSY

- Stay with your child to stop her hurting herself. Lie her on her side on the floor without a pillow. Do not try to restrain her.
- Loosen any tight clothing, but do not be tempted to shake your child back to consciousness or to jam anything between her teeth to stop her biting her tongue – you could break her teeth. Don't give her any fluids either.
- As soon as the fit is over, make sure your child is lying on her side and summon medical help.
- To help your doctor make an accurate diagnosis, note carefully the nature of the convulsion, what, if anything, appeared to trigger it off, how long it lasted and so on.
- If the doctor suspects epilepsy, your child will be referred to hospital for special tests to confirm or refute the diagnosis. These will include various blood tests and tests to monitor the electrical activity of the brain.
- If epilepsy is diagnosed the doctor will prescribe special anti-convulsant drugs to control the condition. Every so often your child will need to attend hospital so that her epilepsy can be monitored. Often it is possible to phase out medication if your child does not suffer any fits over a few years, but do not withdraw drugs without medical advice.

- If your child is diagnosed as suffering from epilepsy you will probably feel shocked. Try to treat your child normally and don't make her feel like a special case. Make sure anyone who looks after her regularly, such as a childminder, babysitter or playgroup leader, knows about her condition and how to deal with it. Have a medic-alert bracelet made and ensure your child wears it, in case she has an attack when you are not there.

For advice and support contact: The British Epilepsy Association, Anstey House, 40 Hanover Square, Leeds, Yorkshire LS3 1BE. Tel: Leeds 439393.

See also: Convulsion.

FEVER (HIGH TEMPERATURE)

Normal body temperature lies between 36 and 37.5°C (96.8 and 99.5°C). If the temperature rises above this it can be a sign of infection. Fever, or raised temperature, is not an illness in itself, but a sign that your child's body is trying to fight off a bacterial or viral infection. Fever often develops a few days before an infectious illness becomes obvious. A child with a fever will often complain of a headache, his skin may be flushed and he appears irritable. He will probably feel thirsty, as a raised temperature will make him sweat more than usual. The height of a fever is no indication of the seriousness of an illness in a baby or small child. You should always consult a doctor if a baby under six months has a fever, if a child's temperature exceeds 39°C (102.2°F), or if your child has a fit (convulsion) brought on by a high temperature.

In addition to the usual infectious diseases, a fever can be a sign of

- ear infection
- tonsillitis, laryngitis, glandular fever
- respiratory infections such as coughs, colds, bronchitis and so on
- urinary infection
- food poisoning

WHAT TO LOOK OUT FOR

- Your child may feel hot and look flushed
- Temperature over 37°C (98.6°F)

- Rapid breathing
- Drowsiness
- Irritability
- Sweating
- Glassy eyes

Make a note of any other symptoms your child has, such as swollen glands, spots, dislike of light, and so on, to help the doctor make a diagnosis.

HOW TO TREAT A FEVER

- See Does My Child Have a Temperature? on pp. 11–13.

See also: Chicken pox; Colds; Convulsion; Cough; Croup; Earache; German measles; Measles; Mumps; Otitis media; Roseola infantum; Scarlet fever; Urinary infection; Whooping cough.

FOOD POISONING

This is a type of gastroenteritis caused by eating contaminated food. Symptoms include colicky pain in the stomach, a raised temperature, vomiting and diarrhoea. Food poisoning can be caused by several different types of germs, such as salmonella, listeria, E.coli, and staphylococci. Alternatively your child may have eaten a poisonous plant or household chemical. Food poisoning is especially serious in a small baby because of the danger of dehydration.

Cases of food poisoning have been on the rise in this country over the last few years due to the revolution in our buying and eating habits. Most families now eat far more ready meals, takeaways and restaurant food than they did a few years ago. Cook-chill foods are an especially likely source of food poisoning as they are not cooked thoroughly enough beforehand to kill off all the bacteria. If they don't reach a high enough temperature for long enough when you cook them at home, any germs present in the food have a chance to multiply.

Whatever the causes of food poisoning, one fact is certain: the very young are among the groups most at danger from its effects.

You can help prevent food poisoning by being scrupulously careful in your storage and preparation of food.

WHAT TO LOOK OUT FOR

- Stomach cramps
- Raised temperature
- Diarrhoea, which may contain blood, pus or mucus
- Vomiting
- Loss of appetite
- Shivering
- Muscle pains

HOW TO TREAT FOOD POISONING

- Observe your child carefully for symptoms.
- Allow her to rest her stomach by keeping off solid food (she probably won't feel like eating anyway) and bottle milk. A breast-fed baby can continue to be fed. Make sure your child drinks plenty of fluids.
- Try to work out what your child has eaten that could have caused the food poisoning. Undercooked eggs, chicken, processed meats, prepacked salads and soft cheeses are all likely culprits.
- Call the doctor if your child cannot keep down fluids, if she is not better within 24 hours or, in the case of a baby, if vomiting and diarrhoea continue for longer than six hours.
- In extreme cases your child may need to be admitted to hospital so that the chemical balance of her body can be restored to normal. She may need a special injection to stop vomiting, and/or a rehydrating drip.
- Be scrupulous about hygiene if your child has food poisoning - it can

---

Hygiene rules

- Keep cooked food in the fridge. Always reheat thoroughly any previously cooked food.
- Don't mix cooked and uncooked foods.
- Don't keep cooked food for more than two days.
- Follow the packet instructions on defrosting frozen food before cooking.
- Avoid cooking and food preparation if you have a cut or open wound on your hand.
- Don't leave warm dishes standing around the kitchen, always cool quickly and put covered in the fridge.
- Check that your fridge is the correct temperature, i.e. below 10°C (50°F).

spread rapidly through the family. Keep her hands clean, and make sure they are thoroughly washed after she has been to the toilet. Use disposable nappies and seal them in a plastic bag after use. Wash your own hands thoroughly after each nappy change.

- After 24 hours without vomiting restart feeding very gradually. Give a bottle-fed baby milk diluted with four times the amount of water. Gradually increase the strength over four days until it is back to normal. A baby who is taking solids should be given fruit or vegetable purées. Avoid milk and milk products for a week after the episode and then reintroduce them very gradually.

See also: Dehydration; Diarrhoea; Fever; Gastroenteritis; Vomiting.

GASTROENTERITIS

This is the most usual reason for babies and small children to suffer diarrhoea. It is caused by an infection – most often a virus called the rotavirus – which leads to inflammation of the gut. The germ can be passed by means of contaminated food, inadequate sterilization of bottles, teats etc., or via germs breathed out by adults who have no symptoms. Gastroenteritis can also occur with flu. The illness brews for 24 to 48 hours, after which your child will experience stomach cramps and a raised temperature. Diarrhoea and vomiting start a few days later and can last from one to three days. As with any illness involving diarrhoea and vomiting there is a danger of dehydration, especially in babies under six months old.

WHAT TO LOOK OUT FOR

- Raised temperature
- Abdominal pains
- Vomiting
- Diarrhoea
- Lack of appetite

HOW TO TREAT GASTROENTERITIS

- Stop solid food and milk (a breast-fed baby can continue to be fed) and give your child frequent sips of plain boiled and cooled water, or rehydrating fluid.

- Be scrupulous about hygiene – make sure your child washes his hands after using the toilet and do the same yourself, and after changing nappies.
- Call the doctor if your child's diarrhoea and vomiting have not stopped after six hours, if he is unable to keep fluids down, or if he shows any signs of dehydration such as dry tongue, not passing water, unusual sleepiness.
- Reintroduce food gradually, avoiding milk and milk products; try well-diluted apple or grape juice.
- In serious cases your child may need to be admitted to hospital.
- Occasionally the symptoms of gastroenteritis persist even though your child is better – this is because of temporary damage to the lining of the gut which makes him intolerant of milk products. A special milk-free diet will usually do the trick. Don't try to introduce this on your own; such a diet should only be followed under the supervision of your doctor or health visitor.

See also: Dehydration; Diarrhoea; Food poisoning; Influenza; Vomiting.

GERMAN MEASLES (RUBELLA)

German measles is a mild infection for a child. However, it can be serious if an expectant mother catches it during the first three or four months of pregnancy, as it may cause abnormalities in the unborn baby such as deafness, blindness and mental handicap. The incubation period is between 14 and 21 days, and the virus is spread by droplet infection as the affected person breathes, coughs and sneezes.

Your child may appear unwell for a few days before the rash develops, but often the rash is the first sign of illness starting behind the ears or on the face then spreading over the rest of the body. This rash consists of pink pinpoints, which may look more like a red splodge than a rash. It lasts for one to five days. The rash is not itchy, and your child probably will not have a temperature. However, she may have a runny nose, and the glands at the back of her neck, and sometimes those in her armpits and groin, may be swollen. German measles is not dangerous in itself, but because of the danger to pregnant women you should keep your child away from playgroup and from anyone you know is pregnant. If you are thinking of becoming pregnant and you are in any doubt whether you have had German measles, make sure you are immunized against it. The new MMR – mumps, measles and rubella – is given to children during their second year. Make sure you keep your child's appointment, for her own sake, and for the sake of any pregnant women she may encounter.

WHAT TO LOOK OUT FOR

- Slight feeling of unwellness, with mildly raised temperature
- Pinpoint pink spots starting on the face and behind the ears and spreading to the rest of the body
- Swollen glands at the back of the neck

HOW TO TREAT GERMAN MEASLES

- No special treatment is needed, but call the doctor to confirm diagnosis.
- If you know anyone who could be pregnant, let them know, and keep your child away from toddler group, playgroup, child health clinic and other public places where she might come into contact with pregnant women.
- There is a very slight risk of encephalitis. Contact the doctor immediately if your child develops a high temperature, complains of a severe headache or stiff neck, or becomes drowsy.

See also: Encephalitis; Rashes.

GLANDULAR FEVER

Glandular fever is a viral infection, otherwise known as infectious mononucleosis. It is most commonly diagnosed in teenagers and young adults, but toddlers get it quite frequently too, though it is generally less severe in their case. It is caused by a virus that inhabits the nose and throat and is passed on by close contact. The incubation period is between 4 and 14 days, and symptoms develop gradually. Lack of appetite, a raised temperature, and a general feeling of being unwell occur, often with swollen glands in the neck, armpits and groin and a severe sore throat. There may be yellow spots on the tonsils or little red spots at the back of the throat, and sometimes there is a rash that starts behind the ears and spreads to the forehead. The disease lasts for two to three weeks, but it often takes several weeks, even months, before the sufferer feels completely well again.

WHAT TO LOOK OUT FOR

- Sore throat or tonsillitis. Tonsils may be covered by a thick white substance or red spots
- Tiredness and general feeling of unwellness
- Raised temperature
- Enlarged glands around the neck, armpits and groin
- Rash
- Sometimes the spleen is swollen and, because the liver is affected also, jaundice may occur

HOW TO TREAT GLANDULAR FEVER

- There is no specific treatment, because viruses cannot be treated with antibiotics. Ampicillin (a type of penicillin) causes an unpleasant itchy rash if given to glandular-fever sufferers.
- A blood test will confirm the diagnosis.
- Let your child rest as much as possible, and treat any fever with the measures outlined on page 96. Avoid rough physical games until he has recovered, he probably won't feel like them anyway.
- Be patient with your child if he takes a while to regain his energy.
- Sometimes the virus is reactivated. Watch out for any recurrence of symptoms and report them to the doctor.

See also: Fever; Sore throat.

GLUE EAR

Glue ear is the popular term used to describe a collection of sticky fluid in the middle ear, which leads from the ear to the throat. The ear is made up of three parts: the outer ear, which ends at the ear drum; the middle ear, a small hollow cavity containing the three bones that carry sound vibrations to the inner ear; and the inner ear. The middle ear is enclosed except for the Eustachian tube. When this tube is blocked, as a result of swelling due to infections such as sinusitis, tonsillitis or otitis media, fluid cannot drain away. This fluid becomes sticky and the tiny bones that transmit sound are no longer able to work properly, causing deafness.

Glue ear is painless but it can lead to permanent hearing loss, so it needs treatment. It tends to become worse after colds and other infections and to improve in the summer months. The severity of hearing loss can vary.

WHAT TO LOOK OUT FOR

- Complaints of pressure in the ear
- Reduced hearing in one or both ears

HOW TO TREAT GLUE EAR

- Report any suspected hearing loss to your doctor, who may prescribe nose drops (because the Eustachian tube leads from the nose to the inner ear) or antibiotics to clear any infection and try to reduce swelling of the Eustachian tube.
- If this does not work your child may be admitted to hospital to have the fluid drained under general anaesthetic. At the same time a grommet – a tiny, hollow plastic tube – is inserted into the ear drum to try and prevent further build-up of fluid and to allow what is there to drain away. The grommet usually falls out 9 to 18 months after the operation, by which time the condition has usually cleared up. However, some children need repeated operations until the glue ear clears up of its own accord at about the age of 9 or 10.
- If the glue ear has arisen as a result of repeated infections the child may need to have her adenoids or tonsils out.
- There is still controversy over whether a child with grommets should go swimming. Be advised by your doctor. It is probably sufficient to make sure that your child wears a bathing hat to stop water entering her ears, and to keep her ears as dry as possible at all times.

See also: Colds; Coughs; Deafness; Earache; Otitis media; Tonsillitis.

HAY FEVER

Hay fever is caused by an allergy to grass, tree or plant pollens. It generally occurs in late spring and summer, and the symptoms are sneezing, a blocked or runny nose, itchy or streaming eyes, and wheezing. A susceptibility to hay fever tends to run in families.

WHAT TO LOOK OUT FOR

- Symptoms of a cold during the summer months
- Symptoms that come and go depending on the time of day and conditions, for example if your child's nose starts streaming after the lawn has been mowed.

HOW TO TREAT HAY FEVER

- Try to work out which particular pollen affects your child. For example, if his symptoms are worse in late spring, it could be tree pollens. If he is most affected when you have just mowed the lawn, grass pollens are likely to be the culprit.
- Be guided by the daily pollen counts that appear in the papers and on the radio during the summer months.
- Try to keep your child away from freshly pollinated air as far as practical. Air-conditioned rooms and swimming pools have low pollen counts.
- Discuss with your doctor the new sprays and drops you can buy over the counter.
- If your child's symptoms are severe seek medical advice.
- Ask your doctor whether he or she advises preventive treatment before the start of the pollen season, in the form of spray or drops.

HEADACHE

If your child complains of a headache it is not usually serious. Some children suffer recurrent headaches or stomach aches, which are often related to anxiety. Headaches often accompany a raised temperature, sinusitis or toothache. In extremely rare instances a headache may be a

sign of encephalitis or meningitis, in which case it will be accompanied
by a fever, intolerance of light, and a stiff neck.

HOW TO TREAT A HEADACHE

- Check for other symptoms, such as earache or toothache. Find out if
  your child is running a temperature or if she has fallen and injured
  her head.
- If your child's temperature is normal, encourage her to get some
  fresh air. If the headache lasts longer than an hour give her
  paracetamol syrup and let her rest in a darkened room for a while.
- Call the doctor if the headache continues for over five hours, if your
  child has a temperature, or if she is vomiting, has a stiff neck, and
  cannot stand the light, or if she has had a head injury.

See also: Earache; Encephalitis; Fever; Measles; Meningitis; Sinusitis;
Toothache.

HEAD LICE

Head lice are minute parasites that live in the hair. The eggs, or nits,
are laid close to the scalp, where they are often overlooked. Once they
are hatched they look small and white, rather like dandruff. However,
unlike dandruff they are not easily brushed off but cling to the hair
shaft. After a couple of weeks the nits hatch and the lice bite the scalp,
causing intense itching. If your child scratches his head, secondary
infection occurs, which is similar to impetigo with yellowish, crusty
sores.

WHAT TO LOOK OUT FOR

- Itchy head, especially in hot weather and after exertion
- Tiny, white eggs clinging to individual hairs

HOW TO TREAT HEAD LICE

- Regular thorough combing is the best prevention.
- Head lice are easily spread in situations where there are lots of
  children, such as toddlers' groups, playgroups, schools and so on.

Since they spread very rapidly the whole family needs to be treated.

- Don't be ashamed or transmit feelings of shame to your child if he gets head lice – they are not a sign that he is dirty. In fact, it has been said that lice prefer clean heads! Do let any groups that your child attends know if your child has lice.
- The chemist will be able to recommend a suitable lotion for getting rid of the lice. These smell quite foul, but are effective. After treatment comb your child's hair with a fine metal comb to get rid of all the eggs. Keep lotions out of reach of your child.

HEAT EXHAUSTION

This can occur if your child becomes too hot, either because of staying out for too long in hot sun or because of running about too much. Your child's temperature rises and her skin becomes hot, pale and clammy. If heat exhaustion is not treated heatstroke can occur.

WHAT TO LOOK OUT FOR

- Pale, clammy skin
- Temperature over 38°C (100.4°F)
- Headache
- Dizziness
- Cramps
- Thirst
- Nausea
- Exhaustion

HOW TO TREAT HEAT EXHAUSTION

- Lie your child down in a cool, shady place – under a tree if you are outside – and remove her clothes.
- Sponge her down with tepid water.
- Give her cool fluids.
- Take your child's temperature after half an hour to check it is coming down. If her temperature has not lowered after an hour, or if she is still hot with a dry skin, take her to the doctor.
- To prevent heat exhaustion make sure your child always wears a hat

and loose cotton clothing when playing out in the sun. Encourage her to come into the shade regularly and to sit down with a cool drink at frequent intervals, especially if she is prone to exhaustion when it is hot.

See also: Heatstroke.

HEAT RASH (PRICKLY HEAT)

Heat rash occurs not, as you might expect, because of being out in the sun, but as a result of the pores leading to sweat glands becoming blocked. Babies are especially prone to heat rash – whether or not the weather is hot – because their bodies are not very good at regulating temperature. The red rash is most often seen on the neck, shoulders and chest and in skin creases. It is not serious, and causes only a mild degree of discomfort.

WHAT TO LOOK OUT FOR

- Tiny red spots in the creases of the elbows, groin, knees or nappy area, and on the cheeks, neck, shoulders and chest
- Flushing of the skin

HOW TO TREAT HEAT RASH

- Keep your baby's skin cool and dry. A tepid bath or a sponge down will help cool him.
- Dress your child lightly in cotton or cotton-mix clothing.
- Check that the heating in your house is not set too high. Turn it down, open a window or use a fan to keep the air cool.
- If the rash does not clear up after 12 hours consult the doctor.

See also: Nappy rash; Rashes.

HEATSTROKE (SUNSTROKE)

Heatstroke is caused when the body's temperature-regulating mechanism breaks down due to excessive heat. When this happens the sweat glands cannot cope, so the body is unable to cool itself. Your child will be extremely hot, but dry, and she may be drowsy and confused.

WHAT TO LOOK OUT FOR

- Extremely high temperature – 40°C (104°F)
- Hot, dry, flushed skin
- Drowsiness or unconsciousness
- Confusion
- Rapid pulse
- No sweating

HOW TO TREAT HEATSTROKE

- Consult the doctor straight away if you suspect heatstroke. In the meantime take your child out of the sun and undress her.
- It is essential to lower your child's temperature. Sponge her down with tepid water and continue to do so until her temperature falls to 38°C (100.4°F). Keep taking her temperature to ensure it is going down.
- Offer your child lots of cool drinks, but none containing stimulants such as cola-type drinks, coffee or tea.
- To prevent heatstroke make sure your child always wears a brimmed hat in the sun. Protect her skin with a high-factor cream or sunscreening lotion. Make sure she does not spend long periods playing in the sun. Encourage her to rest in the shade and make sure she drinks plenty of fluids.

See also: Heat exhaustion.

HEPATITIS

Hepatitis is inflammation of the liver, caused by a virus. There are several different types of hepatitis of which the most common type affecting children is hepatitis A, with an incubation period of 14–42 days. The hepatitis virus is found in the stools and urine of a hepatitis sufferer and spread when these contaminate food and water. It is not usually a serious illness in children but it is extremely contagious, so your child will have to be isolated. Jaundice develops several days after the onset of the illness.

WHAT TO LOOK OUT FOR

- Abdominal pain below right ribs, caused by enlarged liver
- Loss of appetite
- Diarrhoea
- Nausea and vomiting
- Flu-like symptoms – headache, raised temperature, joint pains
- Jaundice – yellowish tinge to the skin and whites of the eyes; dark urine and light-coloured stools

HOW TO TREAT HEPATITIS

- Keep your child away from toddler group, playgroup and other children. Encourage him to rest in bed if he wants to.
- Be scrupulous over hygiene. Make sure your child has his own towel, flannel, dishes and cutlery, and keep these separate from the rest of the family.
- Make sure your child has plenty of sugary fluids or glucose and water to drink.
- The doctor will advise on further treatment, such as a low-fat diet to rest your child's liver.
- If the doctor suspects hepatitis he or she will carry out a blood test to confirm diagnosis. The doctor may suggest that other members of the family have a gamma globulin injection to reduce the severity of the illness if they develop it.
- Expect your child to take a while to recover completely. Extra patience and tolerance are needed if he seems unduly tired and irritable after an episode of hepatitis. Rest assured that he will recover his usual vitality given time.
- Your child will be infectious for a week or more after the onset of jaundice, and the doctor will probably advise keeping him isolated until the jaundice has gone.

See also: Jaundice.

Hernia

A hernia occurs when the soft tissue of the abdomen protrudes through a gap in its muscular wall. The most common type in babies is the *umbilical hernia*, which is noticeable by a round swelling around the navel. As the baby grows older the hernia usually disappears of its own accord. A *groin* or *inguinal hernia* is also common in babies under one year. It happens when part of the intestine slips down the inguinal canal – the gap down which the testicle descends to the scrotum before birth. Again it may heal itself, but there is a risk that the intestine may become trapped and deprived of its blood supply (strangulated), in which case a minor operation will be needed.

WHAT TO LOOK OUT FOR

- A bulge in the groin or the abdomen, close to the navel, that may appear and disappear with coughing, sneezing, crying or other exertion
- Fever, pain or vomiting if the hernia is trapped (strangulated)

HOW TO TREAT A HERNIA

- Many hernias disappear without treatment. Try to push the hernia gently back into the body. If it is hard or will not go back, or if your child is in pain or vomiting, call the doctor immediately.
- If the hernia has become trapped the doctor will refer your child for minor surgery.
- Take your child for regular check-ups to see whether the doctor considers treatment to be necessary.

Hives (NETTLE RASH OR URTICARIA)

The term nettle rash is apt, because hives is an allergic reaction that produces red patches and raised white weals on the skin, as though your child has fallen in a bed of nettles. Most spots fade within a couple of hours, and larger ones disappear after a day or so. The weals appear in crops, which are extremely itchy. Hives is sparked off by many factors, including insect bites, certain drugs such as aspirin, codeine or

penicillin, foods such as strawberries and shellfish, food dyes such as
tartrazine, or contact with some plants such as nettles and primulas.
The condition is not serious but it can be accompanied by swelling of
the lips and eyelids and may affect breathing, in which case your child
will need urgent medical help.

WHAT TO LOOK OUT FOR

- Itchy, red rash
- Crops of white weals, which develop over a period of time and then
  fade to be replaced by a new crop
- Swelling of lips, mouth or inside of throat

HOW TO TREAT HIVES

- Apply calamine lotion to relieve itching. Alternatively apply iced
  compresses or give your child a cool bath. In mild cases the
  condition cures itself.
- If your child's face is swollen, or if swelling is affecting breathing,
  consult the doctor immediately. He or she may prescribe
  anti-histamine medicine to relieve itching or may give your child an
  injection.
- If your child has recurrent hives, monitor his diet to try and pinpoint
  whether a particular food is triggering attacks. Your doctor may refer
  your child to a skin specialist if you cannot isolate the cause
  yourself.

See also: Allergies; Rashes.

HYDROCELE

This is a collection of fluid in the scrotum (the bag of skin containing
the testicles) which causes it to swell. The condition is often there from
birth and worsens over the following few weeks before going down of its
own accord.

WHAT TO LOOK OUT FOR

- Swelling of the scrotum

HOW TO TREAT HYDROCELE

- No treatment needed unless it persists for months or more, in which case simple surgical drainage by needle will be necessary.

HYDROCEPHALUS

Hydrocephalus, also known as water on the brain, is a rare condition caused by an excessive build-up of the fluid surrounding the brain known as cerebrospinal fluid. It can happen when circulation of the fluid is blocked, or when excessive amounts are produced. The excess fluid collects in cavities in the brain, where rising pressure in the skull can cause brain damage if left untreated.

If the condition develops before birth it can be detected by ultrasound and the baby will be delivered by caesarean section because her head will be abnormally large. In such a case she will probably also suffer from spina bifida. If the condition occurs after birth the baby's head may be a normal size at birth but then grow larger, so that the forehead expands and overhangs the face. The baby's fontanelles (soft spots) will be tense and swollen, and the veins on her scalp will stand out. Hydrocephalus may also develop as a result of meningitis or a tumour. In this case the excessive fluid inside the skull raises pressure, causing headache and vomiting.

WHAT TO LOOK OUT FOR

- Overlarge head at birth, or head growing larger than normal over the following months
- Swollen, tense fontanelles
- Veins on the scalp standing out
- Headaches and vomiting (in older child)

HOW TO TREAT HYDROCEPHALUS

- If the condition is not detected before birth it should be picked up during one of your baby's health checks. Alternatively if you suspect something is wrong tell your doctor.
- In mild cases drugs may be prescribed to prevent excessive build-up of cerebrospinal fluid, or an operation to drain the fluid into the

bloodstream may be performed. A fine tube is inserted under anaesthetic and drains the fluid into the abdomen or a vein in the neck. After this your child's head will gradually return to normal size. Four out of 10 babies will develop normal intelligence.

For advice and support contact: Association for Spina Bifida and Hydrocephalus, Tavistock House North, Tavistock Square, London WC1B 9HI. Tel: 01-388 1382.

HYPERACTIVITY

A few years ago it became fashionable to attach the label 'hyperactive' to behavioural problems such as lack of concentration, overexcitability, and other types of unacceptable behaviour such as aggression. Such hyperactivity (the prefix 'hyper' simply means 'too much'), was often attributed to certain food additives. Although hyperactivity never became such a fashionable complaint in this country as it did in America, where some children were put on tranquillizers and sedatives to try and calm them, many parents became convinced that their normal but boisterous children were in fact suffering from a disorder.

If you suspect your child is abnormally active, proceed with caution – who can define 'normal' levels of activity? You should consider consulting the doctor only if your child's activity level is causing problems for him in his relations with others.

The main medical reasons for hyperactivity are brain damage, autism, severe epilepsy and psychological problems. Even with these illnesses there is often a large psychological component to hyperactivity. Drugs may calm your child, but they do not tackle the root of the problem. Many parents with a hyperactive child claim their child has been helped by an additive-free diet. You can find out details about such a diet from the support organization below.

WHAT TO LOOK OUT FOR

- High levels of activity
- Restlessness
- Disruptive behaviour and mood swings
- Clumsiness and lack of co-ordination

- Inability to concentrate
- Inability to sleep for prolonged periods

HOW TO TREAT HYPERACTIVITY

- Some intelligent children need a lot of attention if they are not to become bored and hyperactive. Be prepared to use all your ingenuity to cater for your child's needs.
- Remember most pre-school children get bored, anxious and overactive from time to time.
- Consult a doctor if you really suspect your child is hyperactive, or if any of the other conditions listed apply to him. Your doctor will probably refer him to a paediatrician or psychotherapist for further investigation.
- Your hyperactive child may be very trying at times. Try to treat him as normally as possible, while staying one step ahead and trying to anticipate his need for change and variety. You will benefit from a break from child-minding from time to time.

For advice and support contact: Hyperactive Children's Support Group, 59 Meadowside, Angmering, West Sussex BN16 4BW.

IMPETIGO

Impetigo is a common skin infection caused by the staphylococcus germ, which lives in the nose and on the skin. The child develops small blisters, usually on the face, which burst and crust over to form golden-brown scabs that may ooze fluid. Impetigo is not serious and is quickly cleared up using an antibiotic cream which can be prescribed by your doctor. As it is highly contagious, however, you should keep your child away from other children until the condition has cleared up.

WHAT TO LOOK OUT FOR

- Golden, crusty scabs which may weep, usually on the face, hands, knees or scalp

HOW TO TREAT IMPETIGO

- Pay scrupulous attention to hygiene. Wash your hands before and after applying cream, and encourage your child not to touch the affected area. Cut her fingernails short.
- Report the infection to the doctor, who will prescribe an antibiotic cream which should clear up the rash in about a week. The doctor may also prescribe tablets.
- Gently wash away any crusts before applying cream.
- Make sure your child uses a separate towel and flannel. Check other family members for signs of infection.

INFLUENZA (FLU)

Flu is a viral infection which affects the respiratory tract. Symptoms are similar to those of a cold, together with shivering, aches and pains and a temperature. There is no cure for flu, and it usually clears up on its own within three or four days. However, flu often leaves children feeling weak and depressed, and because the virus depresses the immune system there is a risk of secondary infections such as pneumonia, ear infections, sinusitis, and lung infections.

If your child suffers from lung or heart disease, it is worth having him immunized against flu.

WHAT TO LOOK OUT FOR

- Runny nose and sneezing
- Sore throat and cough
- Raised temperature
- Aches and pains
- Feelings of weakness
- Headache, diarrhoea and vomiting

HOW TO TREAT INFLUENZA

- Keep your child quiet and offer him plenty to drink. Give him paracetamol syrup and any cough medicine advised by your doctor.
- Check for complications, such as a cough that does not appear to be

clearing up, a raised temperature lasting for more than 36 hours, earache, or yellowish or green nasal discharge. If your child has developed a secondary bacterial infection the doctor will prescribe an antibiotic.

● If your child's condition suddenly worsens after he appeared to be recovering, contact the doctor – pneumonia and bronchitis can develop rapidly.

See also: Bronchitis; Cough; Diarrhoea; Headache; Pneumonia; Reye's syndrome; Sinusitis; Sore throat.

INTUSSUSCEPTION

Not many people have heard of intussusception, and yet this condition – in which part of the bowel telescopes into the part in front of it, causing a blockage – is a common cause of stomach pain. It can happen at any age but is most common at about the time a baby is weaned, especially in boys.

Because of muscular spasms the baby cries out in pain and may vomit. At first bowel motions appear normal but as the condition worsens they begin to look like redcurrant jelly, due to blood and mucus. If left untreated the condition can be fatal. However, a simple operation can return the bowel to its normal position.

WHAT TO LOOK OUT FOR

● Spasms of severe, cramplike pain in the abdomen, causing your baby to scream and draw up his legs
● Vomiting
● Pallor
● Raised temperature
● Stools containing blood and mucus

HOW TO TREAT INTUSSUSCEPTION

● If you suspect the condition, contact the doctor at once.
● The doctor will arrange a special X-ray in which a dye is pumped into the rectum to locate the blockage. Sometimes this unblocks the intestine on its own. If not, your baby will need an operation. The

surgeon opens up your baby's abdomen under anaesthetic and pushes
the bowel back from its telescoped condition.

See also: Colic; Diarrhoea; Vomiting.

JAUNDICE

Jaundice is not an illness but a symptom. It is a yellow discoloration of
the skin and eyes, caused by the build-up in the circulation of yellow
bile pigment, or bilirubin. There are several possible causes. The most
common type of jaundice in babies is 'physiological jaundice', which
affects about one-third of babies during the week after birth and occurs
because the baby's immature liver is not yet able to process the waste
products created when red blood cells break down. In some cases
jaundice in newborn babies is caused by a hormone in their mother's
milk – so-called breast-milk jaundice. It is not serious, and it is
perfectly safe to carry on breast-feeding.

Jaundice in a toddler can be caused by hepatitis or certain sorts of
anaemia, in which case the urine is often brown and the bowel motions
are pale.

WHAT TO LOOK OUT FOR

- Yellow skin colour, giving a suntanned appearance
- Yellow-tinged whites of the eyes
- Dark urine and pale stools

HOW TO TREAT JAUNDICE

- Your baby or child should be seen by the doctor in order to
  determine the cause. Any underlying disease such as hepatitis will
  need to be treated.
- In the case of physiological jaundice, make sure your baby has plenty
  of fluids (feed little and often). In more severe cases your baby will
  be placed under a special light (phototherapy) which will help clear
  the jaundice quicker.
- A toddler with jaundice may feel tired and off-colour for several
  weeks, so be patient with him.

See also: Anaemia; Hepatitis.

LARYNGITIS

Laryngitis is inflammation of the voice box and may be caused by a virus or bacterial infection. Symptoms are hoarseness (losing the voice), coughing, possibly croup, a sore throat and perhaps a slight fever. It usually passes off within a couple of days. If your child does develop croup as well you should contact the doctor at once.

WHAT TO LOOK OUT FOR

- Hoarseness/loss of voice
- Dry, hacking cough
- Sore throat
- Slightly raised temperature
- Croupy cough

HOW TO TREAT LARYNGITIS

- The illness often starts at the end of a cold. It is not usually serious unless your child develops a croupy cough or breathing difficulties. Listen out for croup and if necessary call the doctor.
- If your child's temperature rises above 38°C (100.4°F) she could have another secondary infection and needs medical attention.
- Keep the air in your child's room moistened. Use a vaporizer or boil a kettle, and open the window to get some fresh air currents moving in the room. This should help ease the cough.
- Give your child warm fluids such as honey and lemon. Give cough medicine to soothe the cough if advised by your doctor.
- Paracetamol syrup will ease a sore throat and bring down your child's temperature.
- Discourage talking and crying – talk in whispers to your child!

See also: Bronchitis; Cough; Croup; Tonsillitis.

LEUKAEMIA

Leukaemia is cancer of the white blood cells. It is very rare and does not usually strike before the age of three. The causes are not really understood but there is a link with viral infection and exposure to radiation. The white blood cells, which are the body's defence against infection, start to proliferate, and their numbers become out of control. The large number of immature white blood cells lays the child open to infection, and the surfeit of white blood cells leads to a deficit of red blood cells, causing anaemia. Fortunately there are new methods of treatment and the outlook for children with leukaemia is much more hopeful today than it once was.

WHAT TO LOOK OUT FOR

- Loss of energy
- Anaemia/pale skin
- Frequent infections
- Nose bleeds
- Pain in the joints or bruising. Sometimes the child develops a limp
- A purplish-red rash (purpura)
- Bleeding, swollen gums

Do remember it is the combination of symptoms that may indicate leukaemia. If your child has just one or two of the symptoms it is much more likely to be due to an illness of far less significance.

HOW TO TREAT LEUKAEMIA

- Of course leukaemia is not something you can treat unaided. If you suspect leukaemia take your child to the doctor, who will arrange for blood tests and other special tests to confirm the diagnosis and ascertain the type of leukaemia.
- Treatment is by a combination of radiotherapy (X-ray treatment), anti-cancer drugs, blood transfusions and possibly bone marrow transplants. The good news is that with this treatment over half the children with leukaemia can be completely cured and the rest may experience significant remission of the disease.
- Your job is to support your child during treatment and to protect him from infections such as measles and chicken pox, since his lowered defence mechanisms make such illnesses far more serious than they would be normally.

For advice and support contact: Leukaemia Society, P.O. Box 82, Exeter, Devon EX2 5DP. Tel: 0392 218514.

MEASLES

Measles is a highly contagious viral infection, spread by breathing in the germs that cause it. There is a 10-day incubation period between contact with the illness and development of the symptoms. During the first year of life your baby will have some natural immunity to measles, but this later disappears. Measles is not usually serious but it can have serious complications, such as pneumonia, convulsions, otitis media and, in rare cases, encephalitis. Fortunately you can have your child immunized against measles at about fifteen months old as part of the combined MMR – mumps, measles and rubella – vaccine, and it is well worth taking advantage of this.

WHAT TO LOOK OUT FOR

- Symptoms like a bad cold to begin with, i.e. runny nose, cough, slight temperature, watery eyes
- A sharp rise in temperature on the fourth day, it may be as high as 40°C (104°F)
- A brownish-red or coppery rash behind the ears and spreading across the face and the rest of the body
- Eyes sensitive to light
- Small white spots (Koplik's spots) may be noticed inside the mouth

HOW TO TREAT MEASLES

- Contact your doctor to confirm diagnosis.
- Treat any high temperature by tepid sponging and doses of paracetamol.
- Give your child cough medicine, if your doctor advises it, and plenty of fluids.
- Keep your child in a darkened room, if she is sensitive to light.
- Keep your child away from other children until the rash has gone.
- Look out for secondary infections such as earache, as these will need treating. Call the doctor if the cough lasts longer than four days, if your child experiences any difficulty breathing, or if her condition suddenly deteriorates again after she appeared to be recovering.

See also: Colds; Convulsion; Cough; Earache; Encephalitis; Otitis media; Pneumonia.

MENINGITIS

This is a very serious bacterial or viral infection of the membranes
covering the brain and spinal cord. Although the disease is rare it has
been making a comeback in the last few years. Meningitis can strike
suddenly and progress rapidly. Untreated it can lead to brain damage or
death. So if you suspect meningitis do not hesitate to contact the
doctor immediately. Your child may need to be admitted to hospital for
a lumbar puncture – in which some of the spinal fluid is drawn off for
analysis – to confirm or refute diagnosis. If treatment is started at once
the chance of recovery is good.

WHAT TO LOOK OUT FOR

- High temperature
- Headache
- Stiff neck
- Intolerance of bright light
- Drowsiness and vomiting
- Bulging fontanelles in a child under two
- In later stages a purple, blotchy rash and unconsciousness

HOW TO TREAT MENINGITIS

- Viral meningitis sometimes develops following mumps. To check for
  stiffness or pain, see whether your child can touch his chest with his
  chin.
- If you suspect meningitis contact the doctor straight away. The
  doctor will arrange for your child to go to hospital for a lumbar
  puncture. Viral meningitis clears up on its own, whereas bacterial
  meningitis is treated with antibiotic injections.
- Notify anyone with whom your child has been in contact.
- Immunization is available against some types of bacterial meningitis.
  Consult your health visitor for advice if there is an epidemic in your
  area.

See also: Encephalitis; Fever; Headache; Mumps; Vomiting.

Mumps (parotitis)

Mumps is a common infectious illness which causes swelling of the
salivary glands. Children under two are rarely infected. The incubation
period is between 18 and 28 days, and the first signs are that your child
appears slightly unwell, loses her appetite and runs a temperature. After
this the salivary glands in the neck and behind and in front of one ear
start to swell, then a couple of days later the opposite gland swells,
causing earache and pain on eating. Your child will also have a dry
mouth because the salivary glands stop producing saliva. Mumps is
usually a mild disease. The only serious, though rare, complications are
encephalitis and meningitis. Mild complications are abdominal pain
(when the ovaries or pancreas are affected) or pain and swelling in the
testicles. Your child can be vaccinated against mumps during her
second year as part of the MMR – mumps, measles and rubella –
vaccine.

WHAT TO LOOK OUT FOR

- Raised temperature
- Swollen glands behind and in front of the ear and under the chin on
  one or both sides
- Loss of appetite
- Pain on swallowing
- Dry mouth
- Sometimes other swollen glands, e.g. testicles in boys, ovaries in
  girls, which are felt as tenderness low down in the abdomen

HOW TO TREAT MUMPS

- Treat a raised temperature by the measures outlined on page 12.
- Give your child plenty of fluids but avoid anything sour, such as
  lemon juice, as this will cause acute pain.
- A warm compress or a hot-water bottle wrapped in a towel or old
  nappy will help ease pain.
- Call the doctor to confirm diagnosis. Contact the doctor again if the
  illness appears to be getting worse, if your child vomits, or gets a
  headache or stiff neck, if your son's testes are affected or your
  daughter complains of 'tummy ache'.

- Give your child foods that slip down easily, such as soups, milk shakes, blancmange or jelly, and plenty of fluids to drink.

See also: Encephalitis; Fever; Meningitis.

NAPPY RASH

Nappy rash is not serious but it can be extremely trying for babies and their parents. The most usual reason for nappy rash to develop is that the baby is left in his nappy for too long and bacteria in the stools and urine start to break down and irritate the skin. It can also be caused by not drying your baby's bottom well enough after washing, or by an allergic reaction to washing powder or fabric conditioner. If the rash does not clear up after the treatment suggested below it could be a result of thrush or eczema, or because it has become infected, in which case you will need a special cream prescribed by the doctor.

WHAT TO LOOK OUT FOR

- Redness, breaking out into sore spots
- Smell of ammonia

HOW TO TREAT NAPPY RASH

- Leave your baby without his nappy as often as possible, so that air can reach his skin.
- Always cleanse your baby's bottom thoroughly, using baby wipes, water or a mild baby lotion. Change nappies frequently. If you use fabric nappies, place one-way nappy liners inside them to keep his skin dry and allow urine to drain through.
- Use a cream such as zinc and castor oil or a proprietary nappy-rash cream from the chemist.
- If the nappy rash does not start to clear after these measures see the doctor. If the rash is infected or caused by thrush the doctor may prescribe antibiotic ointment.
- Hang terry nappies outside to dry in the fresh air and sunlight as often as possible.
- Do not use plastic pants – the waterproofed fabric type is better.

See also: Allergies; Thrush.

NEPHRITIS

Nephritis is inflammation of the kidney. It sometimes develops after a streptococcal infection such as tonsillitis or scarlet fever. Usually it is mild and most children make a full recovery. However, a few children develop kidney failure, which is why your child will probably be admitted to hospital for bed rest until her kidneys have returned to normal.

WHAT TO LOOK OUT FOR

- Blood in the urine or red, dark-coloured urine
- Passing only small amounts of urine
- Swelling of the face
- Headache
- High temperature
- Loss of appetite

HOW TO TREAT NEPHRITIS

- If you notice the symptoms of nephritis take your child to the doctor. Be especially alert if your child has had impetigo, scarlet fever, or a throat infection such as tonsillitis. The doctor will take blood and urine samples and take your child's blood pressure, which is raised in cases of nephritis.
- Your child will usually be admitted to hospital for rest, and will be given a special diet that does not tax the kidneys. Antibiotics may be prescribed if your child still has traces of the original infection.
- Once your child's urine has returned to normal she can go home, though she will need to have check-ups to ensure that the condition has not become chronic.

See also: Impetigo; Sore throat; Tonsillitis.

NOSEBLEEDS

Nosebleeds occur when blood vessels in the nose burst, perhaps as a result of a knock on the nose or because your child has blown his nose too vigorously, picked his nose, or got a small object stuck up it.

Although a nosebleed looks alarming the amount of blood lost is usually very small. It is only if your child has frequent unexplained nosebleeds or if his nose bleeds after a fall or a blow to the head that you need see the doctor.

HOW TO TREAT A NOSEBLEED

- Sit your child down and squeeze the lower part of his nose firmly, applying equal pressure to both nostrils, where the nose tissue is soft. Continue to do this until the bleeding stops – usually after 10 minutes or so.
- Don't push anything such as cotton wool or a tissue into your child's nose. Keep his head forward to avoid blood dripping down the back of his nose. When the nosebleed has stopped, discourage your child from blowing his nose for at least three hours.
- If your child has suffered a head injury, if the nosebleed carries on longer than half an hour, or if you think your child may have pushed something up his nose, consult the doctor or take your child to casualty. In the case of injury the doctor will arrange for your child to be X-rayed – nosebleeding in these circumstances can be a sign of a fractured skull. If your child has a foreign object in his nose this will have to be removed.
- Recurrent nosebleeds may be due to a weak blood vessel in the nose, which may need to be cauterized (i.e. sealed by heat) under anaesthetic.

See also: Ear problems (listed under Accidents and injuries).

OTITIS EXTERNA

This is an infection of the outer ear canal, and is sometimes known as 'swimmer's ear' because it is more common in children who swim regularly. The infection can be caused by a boil, by a bacterial or fungal infection, or by an object becoming lodged in the ear.

WHAT TO LOOK OUT FOR

- Earache or pain in the ear canal
- Discharge or weeping from the ear

- An eczemalike rash with inflammation, swelling, itchiness and dry, scaly skin

HOW TO TREAT OTITIS EXTERNA

- The illness is not usually serious in itself, but without treatment it may continue for many months or spread further down the ear.
- Check that your child does not have a foreign body in her ear. If she has, take her to the doctor.
- Use soap and water to clean away any discharge from the opening of the outer ear canal. Do not attempt to clean inside the ear canal.
- Consult the doctor, who will examine your child's ears using a special instrument called an otoscope and may gently clean any discharge from inside the ear.
- The doctor may prescribe drops or ointment to put in the ear, or put a special pack into the ear canal itself. If necessary he or she can arrange for your child to be seen by an ear, nose and throat specialist.
- Make sure water does not enter your child's ear during bathing, and do not let her go swimming until the infection has cleared up. Once it has, two or three drops of olive oil in the ear before swimming may guard against recurrence.
- Offer paracetamol syrup to relieve any pain.
- Never poke inside the ears with cotton wool or a cotton bud. It is quite sufficient to wipe away any wax that works its way to the outside of the ear. Wax is normal and in fact helps keep the ears clean and free from infection. Pushing things into the ear to clean it will only push the wax further down and could damage the delicate ear lining, or drum.
- Do not use ear drops unless advised to by your doctor.

See also: Earache; Ear problems (listed under Accidents and injuries); Glue ear; Otitis media.

OTITIS MEDIA

This is an infection of the middle ear. There are several types of ear infection, and they usually cause fluid to build up inside the middle ear

causing earache and deafness. Young children are especially prone to
the condition because the Eustachian tube, which joins the back of the
nose, the throat and ear, is short, making it easy for germs from a nose
or throat infection to reach the ear. It is important to treat otitis media
immediately, otherwise it can lead to permanent deafness.

WHAT TO LOOK OUT FOR

- Crying, fretful baby, who may or may not pull his ear
- Severe earache in a toddler
- Raised temperature of over 39°C (102.2°F)
- Deafness in the affected ear
- Vomiting
- Soft wax or pussy discharge from the ear

HOW TO TREAT OTITIS MEDIA

- The illness lasts between one and four days. Contact the doctor as
  soon as you suspect an ear infection.
- Reduce your child's temperature by giving him cool drinks and
  keeping him cool by tepid sponging if necessary.
- Give paracetamol syrup to relieve pain.
- The doctor will examine your child's ear and, although many ear
  infections are caused by viruses, he or she may prescribe antibiotics
  to clear up any infection, and/or decongestant medicines to relieve
  swelling.
- If your child regularly suffers ear infections he may be referred to an
  ear, nose and throat specialist. Most children with a tendency to ear
  infections grow out of them by the age of five or six, and there is no
  damage to their hearing.

See also: Deafness; Earache; Glue ear; Rheumatic fever.

PNEUMONIA

Pneumonia is inflammation of the lung, caused by either a bacterial or
viral infection. There are several different types of the illness, only
some of which are infectious. These days pneumonia is rarely the killer
it was in the past. It is usually the result of an infection such as a cold or

flu spreading to the lungs. It can also develop following bronchitis, when it is known as bronchopneumonia. This is the type of pneumonia that most often affects babies and toddlers. Lobar pneumonia, in which one lobe, or area, of lung is affected, generally occurs in older children.

WHAT TO LOOK OUT FOR

- Breathlessness. Your child seems to be having trouble breathing and her chest wall may be depressed with each breath. She may make grunting sounds as she breathes, and flare her nostrils
- Dry cough
- Chest pain, which is worse on deep breathing
- Raised temperature up to 39°C (102.2°F)
- Stomach pain

HOW TO TREAT PNEUMONIA

- Be suspicious if your child has had a cold or other respiratory infection that appears to be getting worse instead of better. Children with asthma or cystic fibrosis may be especially susceptible to pneumonia.
- Always contact the doctor. Your child may need to be admitted to hospital, where a chest X-ray will be carried out to confirm diagnosis. If the pneumonia is thought to be bacterial your child will be given antibiotics.
- A small baby may need to be nursed in hospital inside an oxygen tent.
- If you are nursing your child at home, give her plenty of drinks to prevent dehydration. Keep her propped up on several pillows to ease breathing and keep the room well humidified. Once she feels like eating, give her bland foods that are easy to digest.
- Bacterial pneumonia generally lasts a week to 10 days. Viral pneumonias tend to be less serious, and usually clear up within a week. Even so your child may still feel frail for two to three weeks after the illness.

See also: Bronchitis.

POLIO

Polio (poliomyelitis) is a serious viral infection affecting the nerves and spinal cord. It is spread by dust and droplets, and the virus is also carried in an infected person's bowel motions. As with many other viral illnesses, symptoms are rather vague: fever, sore throat, headache, together with a stiff neck or cramping muscle pains. If left untreated polio can cause paralysis of the leg muscles. Today, thanks to vaccination, polio is rare in the developed world, though not elsewhere. The best protection you can offer your child is to make sure he is up to date with his immunization schedule. The polio vaccine is given by mouth.

WHAT TO LOOK OUT FOR

- Sore throat
- Headache
- Vomiting
- Raised temperature
- Weakness, progressing to paralysis in the lower limbs or in the chest, which causes breathlessness
- Stiff neck

HOW TO TREAT POLIO

- Contact the doctor immediately if you suspect polio. Since the disease is caused by a virus there is no drug treatment. However, rest can help and the doctor may want your child to be nursed in hospital, where his breathing can be taken over artificially if necessary.

See also: Fever; Influenza; Sore throat.

PYLORIC STENOSIS

The pylorus is the strong ring of muscles that controls the passage of food out of the stomach and into the intestines. Pyloric stenosis refers to the swelling and narrowing of this muscular ring. It causes forcible (projectile) vomiting, when the food literally shoots out across the room. It is not to be confused with the normal possetting that some babies have after a feed.

The causes of pyloric stenosis are not fully understood. What happens is that whenever your baby has a feed the muscles in his stomach tighten in an effort to make the food pass through the pylorus. As this is impossible, the baby is violently sick. The main danger is that a baby can become rapidly dehydrated, and without treatment could even die.

Fortunately a small operation to open up the pylorus can solve the problem. Contact your doctor if your baby, who has previously seemed perfectly healthy, develops projectile vomiting. It usually occurs between about three and six weeks of age. The illness affects more boys than girls and may be hereditary.

WHAT TO LOOK OUT FOR

- Projectile vomiting after feeds (the vomit comes out in a great gush, and is so forcible it may be projected some metres)
- Constant hunger
- Failure to gain weight
- Vomiting begins usually between your baby's third and sixth week, though it may start as early as the first week, or as late as the twelfth
- Irritable, fretful baby, who is weak from hunger
- No bowel movements
- Pyloric stenosis tends to run in families and affects four times as many boys as girls

HOW TO TREAT PYLORIC STENOSIS

- If your baby vomits the whole feed up forcibly after almost every feed contact the doctor at once. He or she will refer the baby to a paediatrician at the hospital, who will examine the baby, and will probably be able to feel the hard, tight knot of muscles at the lower end of the stomach (upper abdomen). The paediatrician may also be able to see the waves of tightening stomach muscles, passing from left to right. Your baby may need to have a special X-ray in order to confirm the suspected diagnosis.
- If pyloric stenosis is diagnosed your baby will need a minor

operation, which involves making a small cut in the pylorus to open it sufficiently for food to pass through. Occasionally in mild cases non-surgical drug treatment may be tried. Complete cure follows an operation, and within a couple of days your baby should be back to his usual healthy self.

RASHES

Rashes are one of the most common symptoms of the various infectious diseases of childhood. Other common causes include skin ailments, temporary allergies, bites or infestations. Contact the doctor if you suspect one of the conditions listed in the table below, if other clues alert you to problems, if your child has a rash together with a temperature of over 37.8°C (100°F), or if he also has a headache or seems drowsy or confused.

WHAT TO TELL THE DOCTOR

- Make a note of the type of rash – are the spots fine, raised, close together, blistered?
- Whereabouts on the body is the rash?
- Has the rash changed at all, for example have spots turned into blisters?
- Are there any other signs of infection, such as a raised temperature, or other clues to illness?

HOW TO TREAT RASHES

- Keep your child's skin cool to ease itching. Cool baths with bicarbonate of soda added may help. Dress your child in light cotton clothing, and try to prevent him sweating too much.
- Apply calamine lotion or cream to soothe an itchy rash.
- Keep your child's nails short to prevent him scratching. In the case of a baby use scratch mittens or turn down the cuffs of his stretch suit.

See also: Allergies; Hives.

TYPE OF RASH	Possible cause
Small, red, itchy bumps all over body.	Allergy
Small, red lumps appearing in crops all over body and becoming blistered. Intensely itchy.	Chicken pox
Patches of dry, scaly skin that may weep, on face, hands or in skin creases. Itchy.	Eczema
Reddish-brown, non-itchy rash on face and body.	German measles
Coppery rash starting behind ears and spreading over face and rest of body. Little white spots in mouth.	Measles
Small, purplish bleeding spots under the skin that don't fade when you press them and look as if the blood has leaked out under the skin.	Drug reaction; meningitis; hepatitis; leukaemia; some types of anaemia
Red, speckly rash all over the body.	Roseola infantum

What to do

Check whether your child has been in contact with something that may have provoked the rash, e.g. wool, garden plants. Has your child been taking penicillin or other medication, or eating anything such as shellfish or strawberries? Soothe the rash with cool baths and contact the doctor if it doesn't fade within hours.

Does your child have any other symptoms, e.g. fever, headache? Has he been in contact with anyone with the disease? Contact the doctor for confirmation of the diagnosis. Bathe rash in warm water with bicarbonate of soda added. Apply calamine lotion or cream.

Does anyone in your family suffer from eczema, or other allergies? Has your baby just started solids? Consult the doctor.

Check your child's temperature and whether glands at back of neck are swollen. Contact the doctor. Keep your child away from public places. Contact any women in the first three months of pregnancy who may have been exposed to your child.

Child will usually have been unwell for a few days prior to rash, with cold-type symptoms and runny eyes. Call the doctor.

Such a rash, called a purpuric rash, happens as a result of bleeding under the skin. It can occur as a result of sensitivity to a drug your child has taken or to one you took during pregnancy, but in the case of a newborn baby such rashes can be an indication of more serious problems. Check your child's temperature. Does he dislike bright light? Consult the doctor, who will take a blood sample to check for serious causes.

Check temperature – the roseola rash appears as a high temperature falls. Contact the doctor for confirmation.

TYPE OF RASH	Possible cause
Pink, blotchy or scarlet rash all over body, with paler patch around the mouth.	Scarlet fever (Scarlatina)
Irritating, red, raised spots, small blisters and black, slightly raised threadlike spots on palms of hands, soles of feet, head and neck.	Scabies
Itchy, red raised patches and white weals.	Urticaria (nettle rash)

REYE'S SYNDROME

Reye's syndrome is an extremely serious illness which involves swelling of the brain and liver. After a mild respiratory infection, or sometimes following flu or chicken pox, there is a sudden attack of vomiting accompanied by other symptoms, such as irritability, delirium, fits, lack of co-ordination, and a high temperature. In severe cases your child may become unconscious or go into a coma. The causes of Reye's syndrome are unknown, but it is thought that it may be a viral infection. Recently Reye's syndrome has been linked with aspirin. Since this discovery children's aspirin products have been withdrawn from the shops and the number of cases of Reye's syndrome has declined.

WHAT TO LOOK OUT FOR

- Sudden vomiting after another illness such as a cold, flu or chicken pox
- Raised temperature

What to do

Check temperature – it will be about 39.4°C (102.9°F). Has your child been
ill, with a severe sore throat, vomiting, and lack of appetite? Has he been
in contact with children with a throat infection or scarlet fever? Contact
the doctor.

Take your child to the doctor for diagnosis and treatment. Apply special
skin preparation prescribed. Treat others in the family, and wash all
underwear, sheets, pillow cases and so on, to make sure no mites remain.

Has your child been in contact with nettles, or other irritating plants, or
bitten by fleas from a cat or dog? Other causes include virus infections,
allergies to drugs, cow's milk, food dyes or preservatives, or very
occasionally severe mental stress. Contact the doctor, who will try to
track down the cause and may prescribe an appropriate medication.

- Confusion/lack of co-ordination
- Lethargy, unconsciousness, coma

HOW TO TREAT REYE'S SYNDROME

- Take your child's temperature, and if it is raised treat it according to
  the methods outlined on page 12. Do *not* give your child aspirin.
- Contact the doctor, who will be able to confirm the diagnosis. Your
  child will need to be admitted to the hospital intensive care unit
  where she will be given blood tests to confirm diagnosis and if
  necessary a liver biopsy (in which a minute piece of liver is snipped
  off under anaesthetic and analyzed). In Reye's syndrome fatty
  droplets are distributed in the liver in an abnormal way.
- Treatment is aimed at reducing swelling of the brain and correcting
  biochemical abnormalities that have arisen as a result of the illness.
  A glucose and mineral drip will be set up and your child may need to
  be sedated.

See also: Chicken pox; Fever; Influenza; Vomiting.

RHEUMATIC FEVER

In the days before antibiotics, rheumatic fever was a common childhood illness. Today it is rare before three years of age. It develops a week or so after an infection (usually of the ear or throat) caused by the streptococcus germ. It is characterized by inflammation of the large joints (arthritis) and heart (carditis). In the later stages the nervous system may be affected, causing involuntary writhing movements of the arms and legs. This condition used to be known as St Vitus' Dance. Occasionally the disease causes permanent damage to the heart which often doesn't become apparent until later in life.

WHAT TO LOOK OUT FOR

- Fever
- General unwellness
- Painful swelling of the joints, usually the knees and ankles
- Blotchy rash on the body, arms and legs. Hard swellings (nodules) near the joints
- Pain in the chest/breathlessness
- Later on, clumsiness, slurred speech, twitchy muscles, uncontrollable movements

HOW TO TREAT RHEUMATIC FEVER

- If your child develops any of the above symptoms following a sore throat, tonsillitis or an ear infection, check his temperature and feel his knees and ankles to see if he complains of tenderness.
- Contact the doctor. Your child will have to be admitted to hospital for rest and treatment. This consists of treating swollen joints with anti-inflammatory drugs. If your child is suffering heart problems he will be given antibiotics, and if the nervous system has become involved he will be sedated. Your child may have to stay in hospital for a long time.
- Once your child comes out of hospital it will take him a while to recover fully. The doctor will usually advise plenty of rest for six months. Long-term antibiotics may be prescribed to avoid the risk of recurrence. Your child will be checked to see whether there has been any damage to his heart.

- If your child has had rheumatic fever, inform the dentist before any dental treatment. He will need protective antibiotics to avoid the risk of infection, which could affect his heart valves.

See also: Otitis media; Sore throat; Tonsillitis.

RINGWORM

Ringworm is a common fungal infection of the skin and in fact has no connection with worms at all. The infection produces an itchy, red patch of inflammation which may become scaly, and is common in warm, moist areas of the body, such as the groin, feet, scalp, or under the arms. On the scalp the condition causes the hairs to break off, leaving a small, bald or whiskery patch.

WHAT TO LOOK OUT FOR

- Red, itchy, scaly patches of inflammation
- Bald patches on the scalp

HOW TO TREAT RINGWORM

- Consult the doctor, who will prescribe an anti-fungal cream and tablets. The hair will grow back once the fungus is destroyed.
- To avoid reinfection wash all sheets and pillowcases well and replace combs and hairbrushes. Disinfectants and antiseptics do not kill the fungus.
- Ringworm is often caught from pets. If you suspect the family pet is affected take it to the vet.
- Be scrupulous over hygiene to avoid the condition spreading.

ROSEOLA INFANTUM

This is a mild infection which affects children under three. The incubation period is about 10 days, after which a high temperature develops and lasts for about four days. As the temperature falls back to normal a pink or reddish speckly rash appears, first on the body and then spreading to the limbs and neck. The rash fades after a couple of days and the child is better. No one knows what causes roseola but it is probably a virus. It is not serious; the only potential problem is febrile convulsions if the fever rises very high.

WHAT TO LOOK OUT FOR

- Raised temperature for three or four days
- Flat red or pink rash on the body, arms, legs and behind the ears

HOW TO TREAT ROSEOLA

- Bring down your child's temperature using tepid sponging, paracetamol syrup and so on, as detailed on page 12.
- Consult the doctor to confirm diagnosis, and again if your child suffers a convulsion.

See also: Convulsion; Fever; Rashes.

SCABIES

Scabies is a highly infectious skin condition caused by a microscopic mite which burrows into the skin. Symptoms are itchy spots which usually occur between the fingers, on the palms of the hands, soles of the feet and the genitals. Close bodily contact at toddler group or other places where there are lots of children together is the main cause. The itchy spots are a result of the skin's reaction to the mite.

WHAT TO LOOK OUT FOR

- Itchy pimples, which are usually more irritating at night
- Sores or scabs
- Ridges ending in a black spot where the mite burrows in

HOW TO TREAT SCABIES

- Consult the doctor if you suspect scabies. He or she will prescribe an anti-bacterial cream to treat any infection and a special lotion that must be used by the whole family. It is essential to treat everybody in the household as scabies is highly contagious.

- To prevent reinfection, launder all bed linen and clothing thoroughly. Give it a good airing outside if possible, too.
- Inform your child's toddler group or the mothers of any other children with whom your child is regularly in contact.

See also: Rashes.

SCARLET FEVER

Scarlet fever used to be one of the great childhood killer diseases, but today it is much less severe. It is caused by streptococcus bacteria – the same germ that causes tonsillitis and laryngitis. In fact, scarlet fever often starts off with a sore throat, similar to tonsillitis. Two days after the sore throat a rash of tiny red spots appears on the child's face and body. The rash feels rough and turns white when pressed. The face is reddened but the area around the lips is pale. Your child will have a high temperature and feel generally unwell, and he may vomit and go off his food. The rash usually lasts between two and four days, and after it clears the skin may peel. Your child's tongue may be furry and white with little red spots on it, and this is known as strawberry tongue.

Scarlet fever is not serious in itself, but there can be complications. These are rheumatic fever, otitis media and nephritis.

WHAT TO LOOK OUT FOR

- Sore throat
- Rash developing on the chest and neck then the whole body except around the mouth
- White furry tongue with red patches (strawberry tongue)
- Fever
- Inflamed tonsils
- Vomiting

HOW TO TREAT SCARLET FEVER

- Look inside your child's mouth to check the state of his tongue and tonsils. If he has a fever, treat according to the method outlined on page 96.

- Contact the doctor, who may prescribe a course of antibiotics to prevent complications developing. Make sure your child finishes the course.
- Keep your child quiet and offer him plenty of cool drinks. If he has lost his appetite, give him nourishing drinks in the form of milk shakes, a yoghurt drink and so on.
- Soothe a painful throat with paracetamol syrup.
- Watch out for signs that complications may be developing.

See also: Fever; Nephritis; Otitis media; Rheumatic fever; Sore throat; Tonsillitis; Vomiting.

SICKLE-CELL ANAEMIA

This is an inherited condition that affects people of Afro-Caribbean, Indian or Mediterranean origin and is caused by abnormal haemoglobin – the part of the blood that carries oxygen. The red blood cells become sickle-shaped as a result of lack of oxygen, making the blood less likely to clot. The condition is carried by a recessive gene – both parents are carriers but they are not affected by the disease themselves. If there is a family history of sickle-cell anaemia you will be offered genetic counselling when you start a family.

WHAT TO LOOK OUT FOR

- Symptoms do not occur until six months after the onset of the disease. After that the child has 'crises' in which large numbers of red blood cells break down, causing painful swollen joints in the hands and feet
- Severe abdominal pain following damage to blood vessels in the spleen
- Jaundice
- Anaemia
- Fatigue
- Slow growth

HOW TO TREAT SICKLE-CELL ANAEMIA

- During a crisis painkilling drugs and bed rest are advised.

- Encourage your child to drink plenty of fluids, as dehydration makes the condition worse.
- The doctor will probably advise vitamin supplements.
- Infections and high altitude can spark off a crisis. Make sure your child is fully immunized and keep her away from children with infections. Pay careful attention to your child's diet.
- If the anaemia becomes severe a blood transfusion may be necessary.
- Penicillin may be prescribed to prevent damage to the spleen, which makes your child more likely to succumb to frequent infections.

For advice and support contact: Sickle Cell Society, Green Lodge, Barrett's Green Road, London NW10 7AP.

See also: Anaemia.

SINUSITIS

This is an infection in the sinuses, which are the spaces around the eyes and nose. The sinuses are lined with mucus membranes, so infections of the nose and throat spread easily to them. Sinusitis is rare in babies and small children.

WHAT TO LOOK OUT FOR

- Pain and swelling in the sinuses following a cold
- Yellow-green discharge from the nose
- Pain, redness and swelling around the eyes
- Blocked nose
- Pain on moving the head

HOW TO TREAT SINUSITIS

- In mild cases give your child paracetamol syrup to alleviate pain and discomfort.
- Keep your child's room cool and moist, as a hot, dry atmosphere will worsen symptoms.
- Taking decongestant nose drops or inhaling menthol dissolved in boiling water will help clear your child's nose.
- If the pain is severe, if your child develops a fever, or if the eyelids

become red and tender, seek medical advice. The doctor will usually take an X-ray of the sinuses and prescribe an antibiotic and decongestant nose drops.
- In severe cases your child may need to be referred to an ear, nose and throat specialist, who will drain the sinuses of infected mucus and prescribe antibiotics.

See also: Colds; Cough; Hay fever; Sore throat.

SORE THROAT

A sore throat is usually an indication of an infection, and may accompany a cold or flu. If your child has mumps she may also complain of a sore throat. Streptococcal bacteria are responsible for many sore throats and can sometimes set up a serious reaction in other parts of the body (see Nephritis and Rheumatic fever). In fact if your child has a sore throat she may not complain about that as such but will appear generally unwell and may go off her food or have difficulty swallowing. A baby may take a few sucks from bottle or breast and then break off crying.

WHAT TO LOOK OUT FOR
- Pain in the throat
- Problems swallowing
- Swollen glands
- Irritability

HOW TO TREAT A SORE THROAT
- Look at your child's throat to see if you can detect any inflammation. Take her to the window or under an angled lamp, press down her tongue with a spoon handle and tell her to say 'aagh'.
- Check the glands at the side of her neck and under her chin for swelling; and take her temperature.
- Treat the sore throat with cool drinks and paracetamol syrup. Your child may like to take sips of honey and lemon.
- Give your child bland, easy-to-swallow foods such as egg custard, blancmange, yoghurt, or milk shakes.

- Call the doctor if your child seems very ill, if she develops trouble with breathing, if she also has a high temperature, or if she develops a fine red rash and you know she has been in contact with someone with tonsillitis or a sore throat. The doctor may take a swab to see whether the sore throat is caused by streptococcus bacteria and prescribe antibiotics.

See also: Colds; Influenza; Laryngitis; Mumps; Nephritis; Rheumatic fever; Scarlet fever; Tonsillitis.

SQUINT

Up to the age of six months many babies momentarily cross their eyes, or squint, when they are trying to focus on something. Older babies sometimes appear to squint, especially if they have a broad nose, which makes their eyes appear to turn in. A true squint, or strabismus, occurs because of some imbalance in the eye muscles. This is often because of long sight, which makes focusing on nearby objects difficult. The child turns in his eye in an attempt to focus. It can also be due to short sight, and in some cases the cause is simply not known.

Whatever the cause of squinting it is essential that a baby whose eye turns in or wanders should be checked by a doctor. Left untreated, a squint can have serious consequences. If both eyes are pointing in different directions double vision occurs. In order to correct this the brain suppresses the image from one eye, which leads to loss of vision in the 'lazy eye'. If your baby over six months appears to be squinting, don't ignore it; see the doctor.

WHAT TO LOOK OUT FOR

- Eyes that appear to be looking in two directions, are crossed, or wander

HOW TO TREAT A SQUINT

- If you suspect a squint take your child to see the doctor. He or she will perform a few simple tests to check your child's eyesight, and if necessary will send your child to see an eye specialist.

- The treatment consists of blocking out the child's 'good eye' with a patch, in order to force the muscles in the lazy eye to strengthen. If the squint does not correct itself your child may need a small operation to readjust the muscles around the outside of the eyeball. Provided the squint is corrected before your child is four years old there is an extremely good chance that his sight will be normal and permanent damage will be avoided.
- Your child may also have to wear special glasses.

STICKY EYE

A sticky eye is a common minor infection in newborn babies. It is usually caused by amniotic fluid, blood, or the chemicals used for swabbing you down during birth, getting into the baby's eye and causing inflammation. Often the sticky eye gets better without treatment within a day or so. However, if the eye starts to ooze a yellow discharge (pus) this is an indication that infection is present, which will need to be treated with eye drops or an antibiotic ointment.

WHAT TO LOOK OUT FOR

- Inflammation and stickiness of the eye
- Yellow discharge weeping from the eye
- Reddened eyeball

HOW TO TREAT A STICKY EYE

- Your midwife will show you how to swab your baby's eyes using warm, boiled water and a piece of cotton wool (see below).
- When you lie your baby down to sleep place him with the unaffected eye against the sheet so that he does not pick up infection in the good eye from matter that has dripped on the sheet.
- Consult the doctor if your baby's eyeball is red and there is pus oozing from his eye. The doctor will prescribe eye drops or ointment to be applied in a thin strip along the lower eyelid, and may also take a swab to check on the type of bacteria causing the infection.
- Be scrupulous over hygiene. Change your baby's bedding frequently.

To avoid spreading infection, do not use the same piece of cotton wool for cleansing both eyes.
- A drop of expressed breast-milk applied directly to the baby's eye often miraculously clears it up.

How to swab your baby's eyes
1. Take a piece of cotton wool and dip it in warm, sterile water.
2. Gently wipe your baby's eye from the inside corner outwards (i.e. away from the bridge of the nose).
3. Discard swab.
4. Take a fresh piece of cotton wool and repeat with other eye.
5. Wash your hands thoroughly.

See also: Conjunctivitis.

STYE

A stye is an infection of the hair follicles from which the eyelashes grow. It starts off as a light-red swelling, comes to a head over the course of four or five days, then bursts. There is no need to consult the doctor unless your child suffers from recurrent styes, in which case the doctor may prescribe an antibiotic ointment as a preventative measure.

WHAT TO LOOK OUT FOR
- Inflammation of the lower, or sometimes upper, eyelid, which becomes swollen with pus over the course of a few days

HOW TO TREAT A STYE
- Once the stye starts to come to a head apply warm compresses. Do this by soaking a pad of cotton wool in hot water and applying it to the stye for about 10 minutes every two to three hours.
- Once the stye has come to a head you can release the pus by gently pulling out the eyelash in the centre of it with a pair of tweezers. If that doesn't work, continue with the hot bathing and the stye should clear up on its own in a couple of days.

- If the stye has not improved in four or five days, or if the eyelid itself swells or the eye becomes red or infected, see the doctor, who will prescribe an antibiotic ointment.
- Be scrupulous over hygiene. Make sure your child has her own separate towel and flannel. Wash your hands after bathing the stye, and make sure your child keeps her hands clean too and avoids touching the stye.

See also: Boils; Conjunctivitis.

SUNBURN

Sunburn is a real burn, caused by exposure to the ultra-violet rays of the sun. We now know that excessive exposure to sunlight during childhood is a factor in the later development of skin cancers, especially in people with fair or freckled skins. Babies and small children have extra-sensitive skins and can be affected even by weak sunlight, especially near water or snow, where the rays are reflected. Protect your child against sunburn by making sure she always wears a hat and a long-sleeved shirt or T-shirt when she goes out in the sun. Protect any exposed areas with a high-factor sunscreen cream or lotion. Acclimatize your child gradually to the sunshine by increasing the amount of time she spends in the sun by 10 minutes each day. If at any time her skin shows signs of pinkness, cover her up or take her out of the sun at once. If your child is in the sea or a paddling pool, reapply sunscreen each time she leaves the water.

WHAT TO LOOK OUT FOR

- Pink or reddened skin
- In more severe cases, pain, irritability, blistering

HOW TO TREAT SUNBURN

- Apply cool compresses, calamine lotion or cream, or aloe vera-based lotion to cool and soothe sunburn.
- Keep the sunburnt areas covered when your child is out of doors. Inside, exposure to air will aid healing.

- If your child seems unwell, is sick or has a raised temperature consult the doctor. He or she will probably prescribe an anti-inflammatory ointment to ease swelling and help the sunburn heal more quickly. If your child's skin has blistered, this means she has a second-degree burn and needs medical attention.
- Give your child paracetamol syrup to ease the pain.

SWOLLEN GLANDS

The first symptom of many infections is that the lymph glands in the neck, groin or armpits swell. The lymph glands are one of the body's main defence mechanisms against infection. When an infection occurs extra white blood cells are produced and travel to the lymph glands nearest the site of infection, causing the glands to swell and feel tender. For instance, if your child has a throat infection the glands below his ear and jaw will swell. This is evidence that the body is doing its job of fighting off the infection. Consult the doctor if the glands remain swollen for over three weeks, or if the glands are red and painful.

WHAT TO LOOK OUT FOR

- Swollen glands behind the ear, below the ear and jaw, in the back of the neck, or in the groin or armpits
- Redness, tenderness
- A raised temperature

HOW TO TREAT SWOLLEN GLANDS

- Most swollen glands do not need treatment but the infection that is causing them may need to be treated. However, if swollen glands persist, especially if they continue to be sore, or if your child has earache, problems breathing, or difficulty swallowing, contact the doctor, who will prescribe antibiotics.

See also: Glandular fever; Tonsillitis.

TEETHING

The age at which the first tooth appears varies widely from one baby to another, but the average age is about six months. Some babies seem to produce teeth completely effortlessly. Others dribble, chew on everything in sight, cry and whinge, and give their parents sleepless nights. Contrary to popular belief, teething does not cause a raised temperature, rashes, diarrhoea, vomiting, breathing problems, or convulsion. If your baby experiences any of these symptoms don't attribute them to teething – take her to see a doctor.

WHAT TO LOOK OUT FOR

- Dribbling
- Reddened gums
- Desire to chew on anything and everything
- Crying and whining
- Inability to sleep
- Reddened cheek or sore patch from constant dribbling

HOW TO TREAT TEETHING

- Comfort and distraction are the best ways to deal with teething. Comfort your baby by giving her extra breast feeds, or a dummy if she has one.
- Biting on something hard will help alleviate discomfort. Try a water-filled teething ring, a bone with a few bits of meat clinging to it, a stick of carrot, or a wedge of apple. Stay with your baby in case she chokes.
- Try rubbing the tender gum with your finger. You can buy teething gels that contain a local anaesthetic. However, these tend to have only a short-term effect because they are rinsed away in the baby's saliva.
- If your child is having trouble sleeping at night, a dose of paracetamol syrup before bed will lessen the pain.
- See the doctor if the symptoms of teething are associated with other signs of illness such as a raised temperature or lack of appetite. Your baby could have an ear or urinary infection that needs treating.

TESTICLES, TORSION

Torsion, or twisting, of the testicle cuts off the blood supply to the testicle. It is fairly rare, especially in small children, but if your child complains of pain in the testicles see the doctor. If the condition is not treated it can cause the testicle to shrink and lead eventually to infertility.

WHAT TO LOOK OUT FOR

- Severe pain or tenderness. If the testicle has not descended the pain may be felt in the abdomen
- Swelling of the testicle, or withdrawal of the testicle into the abdomen

HOW TO TREAT TORSION OF THE TESTICLE

- See the doctor immediately. If the condition is detected early enough, the doctor may be able to twist the testicle back into place. If not, a simple operation will be carried out to put the testicle back to normal.

TESTICLE, UNDESCENDED

The testicles normally descend into the scrotum before birth. They are kept there because sperm needs to be stored at a lower-than-normal body temperature. If a testicle does not descend, this can cause reduced sperm production or infertility. In about two out of 100 babies the testicles are undescended at birth, but normally they do come down in the first few months of life. Immediately after your baby is born the testicles will be drawn up into the scrotum as a reflex if they are cold. If the testicle does not eventually descend, a small operation will be necessary between the ages of two and four to bring it into its normal position.

HOW TO TREAT AN UNDESCENDED TESTICLE

- When your baby has his first check-up before leaving hospital, the paediatrician will examine his genitals to see if his testicles have descended into the scrotum. If one or both are undescended they will probably come down of their own accord over the next few weeks. Try feeling gently for them in the scrotum with warm hands from time to time. The paediatrician will probably suggest a follow-up check some months later to see if they have descended.

- If the testicles have failed to descend by the age of one year, the doctor will suggest that your child goes into hospital for an operation. Your child will usually be allowed to go home on the same day. All you need to do is ensure that he does not engage in active games in the days after the operation, for fear of hurting his scrotum.

See also: Testicles, torsion.

TETANUS

The bacteria that cause tetanus lie in soil, animal manure and rusty metal. They enter the body through a cut and attack the nervous system, causing the muscles of the body to go into spasm. The first muscles to be affected are often those of the jaw, hence the name 'lockjaw'. Tetanus is very serious because if the breathing muscles go into spasm your child could die. The best protection is to make sure your baby is up-to-date with her immunizations. The 'triple' vaccination – diphtheria, whooping cough and tetanus – will provide protection against the illness. Your child should have a booster jab every five years until she leaves school and every ten years after that.

WHAT TO LOOK OUT FOR

- Muscle stiffness, spasms
- Cramp around the jaw and mouth
- Difficulty swallowing or breathing
- Convulsions

HOW TO TREAT TETANUS

- Clean all wounds with soap and water to remove any dirt.

- If it is over six months since your child's last tetanus injection take her to your GP or the hospital for advice about a booster.
- If your child develops any of the symptoms listed above take her to the doctor immediately. The doctor will thoroughly clean the wound and may give her an injection of anti-tetanus globulin to neutralize the toxin produced by the tetanus bacteria. If the disease does develop your child will have to be treated in hospital.

See also: Bites and stings; Cuts and grazes (both listed under Accidents and injuries).

THALASSAEMIA

Thalassaemia is an inherited type of anaemia caused by an abnormal form of haemoglobin – the blood's oxygen carrier. In thalassaemia, which mainly affects those of Mediterranean and South-East Asian origin, the red blood cells become weakened and break down. If both parents carry the faulty gene either of them may suffer a mild form of the disease, but there is a one in four chance the child will suffer from it. The problem becomes apparent when the child is about six months old, with symptoms such as pallor, listlessness and poor feeding. The spleen enlarges in an attempt to produce extra red blood cells, resulting in a swollen abdomen.

WHAT TO LOOK OUT FOR

- Fatigue
- Breathlessness
- Pallor of lips, tongue and extremities
- Loss of appetite
- Swollen abdomen
- Listlessness

HOW TO TREAT THALASSAEMIA

- Prevention is better than cure; if you are at risk of thalassaemia you should be offered genetic counselling and special screening tests during pregnancy to see whether your child will be affected.

- If you suspect your child has inherited thalassaemia, consult your doctor, who will carry out a blood test to confirm diagnosis.
- In severe cases, frequent blood transfusions are necessary to combat anaemia, and drugs are given to prevent the build-up of large amounts of iron in the body which can damage vital organs.
- Bone marrow transplants can be performed to re-establish the manufacture of haemoglobin.
- Occasionally the spleen is removed, either because it has grown so large it is causing problems, or to reduce the need for frequent transfusions.
- Encourage your child to live as normal a life as possible, but avoid contact sports which carry the risk of rupturing the spleen and causing severe bleeding.
- Although the severest form of thalassaemia is fatal, mild forms do not usually cause problems, and the recent development of bone marrow transplantation has improved treatment of the more severe forms.

For advice and support contact: United Kingdom Thalassaemia Society, 107 Nightingale Lane, London N8 7QY.

See also: Anaemia.

THREADWORMS

Threadworms are parasitic worms that live in the intestines. The eggs enter the mouth in contaminated food or via the fingernails, where your child may have picked them up from another child. They then hatch, and the female worm comes out at night to deposit her eggs around your child's anus. This is intensely irritating and if your child scratches, the eggs get under her fingernails and from there to her mouth, when the whole cycle can begin again. Eggs can reside in nightclothes and bedding for two to three weeks.

WHAT TO LOOK OUT FOR

- Itching around the anus at night
- Complaints of stomach ache

- White threads which are often wriggling in the stools or around the anus
- Inability to sleep because of irritation

HOW TO TREAT THREADWORMS

- If your child complains of itching or is finding it difficult to sleep because her bottom is irritated, inspect her anus with a torch and you will probably be able to see the worms, which look like tiny, wriggly white threads. If you examine your child's bowel motions you may also see worms in them. The worms sometimes work their way into a little girl's vagina, causing itching and sometimes soreness and a vaginal discharge.
- If you suspect worms, take your child to see the doctor, who will prescribe a special powder which kills the worms so that they are passed out in your child's stools. The treatment is repeated 14 days later to prevent reinfestation from any eggs that have hatched in the meantime. Everyone in the family should be treated, as the worms spread rapidly from person to person.
- To break the cycle of infection be scrupulous about hygiene. Thoroughly wash night clothes and bed linen, and clean your child's room with a vacuum cleaner. Keep your child's fingernails short, and encourage her to wash her hands after visiting the lavatory. Put your child in a tight pair of pants at night, so that if she scratches she doesn't pick up any eggs.
- Bathe your child every morning and brush her fingernails.

THRUSH

Thrush is a fungus which thrives in moist, warm conditions. It normally lives on the skin and in the bowel, but if it becomes out of control it can cause an itchy skin infection, which in babies is seen in the mouth or the nappy area. It is not known why babies get thrush, but it could be that it comes from the mother's vagina during birth. If you have an attack of thrush – the symptoms are an itchy, cheesy discharge – see the doctor for treatment so you can avoid passing it on to your baby.

WHAT TO LOOK OUT FOR

- Furry white patches covering your baby's cheeks and tongue which won't rub off easily (as milk residue does), and which create sore, bleeding patches when rubbed
- Resistant nappy rash
- Crying and pulling away while feeding, due to mouth soreness

HOW TO TREAT THRUSH

- If your baby has symptoms of thrush consult the doctor, who will prescribe anti-fungal drops for your baby's mouth or anti-fungal cream for nappy rash caused by thrush.
- Put your child into disposable nappies, if he has thrush in the nappy area, until it has cleared up. Meanwhile thoroughly sterilize and wash all his nappies. Change them often and leave his bottom exposed to the air, or put one-way nappy liners inside his nappy.
- Give him liquid food until the thrush has cleared up. Carry on breast- or bottle-feeding as normal. If you are breast-feeding your nipples may have become sore, in which case they need to be treated with anti-fungal medication. If your baby is weaned, yoghurt is a good food to give him as it will help re-balance the bacteria in his body.

See also: Nappy rash.

TIC

A tic is any twitchy, jerky body movement, and often appears when a child is overanxious. Tics are common, and are not a sign of any serious disease. In fact, they often disappear of their own accord.

WHAT TO LOOK OUT FOR

- Twitching
- Blinking
- Headbanging
- Sniffing
- Clearing the throat

HOW TO TREAT A TIC

- The important thing is not to show excessive anxiety over your child's habit. If you pay undue attention to a tic you will probably just prolong its duration.
- Tics usually become worse if your child is overtired or under stress. Make sure she has enough sleep at night and a rest during the day.
- If you know there are particular stresses in your child's life, for example a house move, divorce, the arrival of a new brother or sister, give her lots of love and reassurance.

TONSILLITIS

Tonsillitis is inflammation of the tonsils, two glands that lie on either side of the back of the throat. Tonsils are part of the lymphatic system, contributing to the body's defence mechanisms by trapping any germs that enter the throat in order to prevent them moving to the respiratory tract or the ears. Tonsillitis causes a severe sore throat and raised temperature. Babies under one year old rarely suffer an attack, but some children have frequent bouts of tonsillitis which they usually grow out of by the age of 10. Not so long ago it was the fashion to remove tonsils by surgery, but today this is not done so often.

WHAT TO LOOK OUT FOR

- Sore throat with swollen red tonsils, often with yellow spots
- Raised temperature
- Swollen neck glands
- Coated tongue and bad breath

HOW TO TREAT TONSILLITIS

- Consult the doctor, who may take a throat swab to try and identify the germ causing the tonsillitis. If your doctor suspects a bacterial infection he or she may prescribe antibiotics. If the infection has been caused by a virus, however, antibiotics will have no effect.
- Give your child plenty of cool fluids to drink. Mash or purée his food if he is having difficulty swallowing, and give him bland, easy-to-swallow foods such as blancmange, jelly and yoghurt.

- Paracetamol will ease the soreness and bring down your child's temperature if it is raised.

Should my child's tonsils be removed?

The doctor may advise that your child have his tonsils and adenoids removed if your child suffers recurrent tonsil infections which are also affecting his adenoids and causing frequent middle ear infections, or if recurrent bouts of illness are interfering with his growth and development. Today tonsillectomy, as the operation is called, is much less readily performed than it was in the past, as research has proved that most children grow out of tonsillitis. The operation is performed in hospital under general anaesthetic. However, such an operation does not always cure a recurrent sore throat. Before agreeing to the operation you should discuss with the surgeon whether it would be wise for your child to have his tonsils out, since the tonsils are a first line in the body's defence system.

See also: Earache; Fever; Nephritis; Otitis media; Rheumatic fever.

TOXOCARIASIS

This is an increasingly common infection caused by a type of parasitic roundworm that lives in the gut of dogs and cats. Its eggs are passed out in the animals' bowel motions, and can be picked up on a child's hands, for example while playing in soil in the garden or park. Often the child has no symptoms and you may not even know she has the infection. In a few rare cases it can cause serious eye disease, which can even result in loss of sight. The symptoms are the vague ones that are associated with many childhood illnesses, such as fever, stomach ache, lack of appetite, and skin rashes. If your child suffers any of these, especially if she has been playing in the park, see the doctor.

WHAT TO LOOK OUT FOR

- Lack of appetite
- Slightly raised temperature
- Complaints of stomach ache
- Vision problems

HOW TO TREAT TOXOCARIASIS

- Take your child to the doctor, who will do simple blood tests or may take a sample of her bowel motions for testing. If your child is infected the doctor will prescribe a special drug and advise you to keep her away from animals.
- Make sure any household pets are regularly dewormed. Encourage your child to wash her hands after playing with animals.
- Discourage your child from playing near soil that may contain the faeces of dogs and cats. Take care to cover all sand pits where cats and dogs might foul. Train pets to defecate in a particular part of the garden that is not used by the rest of the family.

See also: Threadworms.

TRAVEL SICKNESS

The movement of a vehicle, be it car, boat, plane or fairground ride, disrupts the balance mechanism in the ear, causing nausea and vomiting. Some children are more prone than others to travel sickness, which often comes on suddenly at about the age of 18 months, but most children grow out of it as they get older.

WHAT TO LOOK OUT FOR

- Nausea and vomiting
- Sweating
- Pallor
- Dizziness
- Drowsiness
- Stomach pain and diarrhoea

HOW TO TREAT TRAVEL SICKNESS

- If your child is quiet and appears drowsy and sweaty, stop the car and let him walk around for a while.
- Allow frequent stops on a long journey so your child can enjoy some fresh air. Provide distractions, such as sing-alongs, story tapes and so on, but do not let him look at a book because this tends to make the

sickness worse. Your child will probably feel better if you position him so he can see out of the front window, to reduce the sensation of motion.

- If your child regularly suffers travel sickness, buy an over-the-counter sickness remedy, which can be taken a short while before you set out. These remedies are very effective, though drowsiness is often a side effect.
- If you have a meal before you go out, make sure your child does not eat too much. Equally, travelling on a completely empty stomach may trigger off an attack of nausea. Take drinks with you, and possibly a small cache of non-greasy snacks such as dried fruit and apples for him to nibble on throughout the journey.
- Take some boiled sweets or mints to reduce the feeling of nausea and to take away the taste of vomit if your child does have the misfortune to be sick.
- Keep the car window slightly open and don't smoke in the car. Carry plastic or brown paper bags for your child to be sick in if necessary.
- In very rare instances severe, prolonged vomiting can cause dehydration, in which case your child will need medical attention.

See also: Dehydration; Vomiting.

UMBILICAL CORD INFECTION

After your baby is born you will be shown how to clean the stump where her umbilical cord was attached. Sometimes this becomes infected, causing it to become red, swollen and sore with a pus-like discharge.

WHAT TO LOOK OUT FOR

- Red, swollen stump
- Oozing pus which may crust over

HOW TO TREAT UMBILICAL CORD INFECTION

- Keep an eye on the stump for signs of infection. The midwife will examine it daily to check that it is healing. If it starts to get red after your baby has been discharged from hospital, contact the doctor.

- The doctor will prescribe an antibiotic cream or powder to apply to the stump. Make sure you keep the stump clean, and swab it with cotton wool dipped in surgical spirit after baths and at every nappy change.
- Salt-water baths will aid healing. Dry the stump carefully afterwards.
- Try to fold nappies, or use disposable ones, so they don't cover the stump – bacteria thrive in warm, soggy conditions.
- In very rare cases if the infection spreads your baby may need to be admitted to hospital for treatment.

URINARY INFECTION

Urinary tract infection is caused by bacteria travelling through the urethra, the tube that leads from the bladder, to the bladder itself and occasionally reaching the kidneys. Urinary infections tend to affect more girls than boys because a girl's urethra is shorter, so it is easy for germs to pass on to the bladder. Occasionally a urinary infection is a result of a blockage or other abnormality of the urinary tract. Your child will have all the usual symptoms of being unwell, and in addition will need to empty his bladder often and will experience pain or burning on doing so. You should always contact your doctor as, if the infection spreads to the kidneys and is left untreated, permanent damage could occur.

WHAT TO LOOK OUT FOR

- Pain or burning sensation on urination
- Frequent passing of urine
- Cloudy unpleasant-smelling urine
- Raised temperature up to 41°C (105.8°F)
- Vomiting
- Abdominal pain and back pain
- Shivering
- Lethargy

HOW TO TREAT A URINARY INFECTION

- If you suspect a urinary infection, take your child to see the doctor.

He or she will probably ask for a specimen of your child's urine, to send away to the hospital laboratory where the bacteria involved can be identified. Urinary infection can sometimes be a first sign of diabetes, so the specimen will also be tested for sugar.

- Treatment consists of a short course of antibiotics. While your child is being treated, make sure he has plenty to drink in order to dilute the urine and keep his kidneys flushed through.
- Give paracetamol syrup for pain relief. To help keep your child's urine alkaline, so that it stings less, give him plenty of lemon barley water, either as a squash or preferably made at home by boiling a handful of barley in 1.2 litres (2 pints) of water for 20 minutes and straining, before adding lemon juice and sugar to taste.
- Give your child a hot-water bottle to hold over his abdomen or back if he is suffering pain there.
- Show your daughter how to wipe her bottom from front to back so that germs from the anus do not enter the urethra.
- If your child suffers repeated urinary infections he will probably have to be seen by a paediatrician, who may arrange for an ultrasound examination of the kidneys or a special X-ray called an intravenous pyelogram, to see whether there are any anatomical abnormalities that are making him prone to infection.

See also: Fever.

VAGINAL DISCHARGE

A little bloodstained discharge in a newborn baby girl is due to the withdrawal of the mother's circulating hormones after birth. A discharge in an older baby or toddler can be due to an infection, threadworms entering the vagina, or occasionally because your child has pushed a small object into her vagina. See the doctor if your child has a persistent or profuse discharge, if she has a bloodstained discharge, or if she experiences pain on urinating.

WHAT TO LOOK OUT FOR

- Thin, yellowish-green discharge
- Signs of threadworms (see page 152)
- Unpleasant-smelling or blood-streaked vaginal discharge

HOW TO TREAT VAGINAL DISCHARGE

- Take your child to the doctor, who will examine her and may take a vaginal swab to see if a particular bacterium is responsible for the discharge. Often it is caused by bubble baths, detergents or fabric conditioners which are setting up irritation.
- Bathe your child in plain water, with perhaps a handful of salt added to soothe irritation and aid healing.
- If the discharge continues and your child has inserted a foreign body into her vagina she will need to have it gently removed by the doctor.
- Any infection will be treated with antibiotics, and the doctor may prescribe a soothing cream to alleviate soreness or irritation.

See also: Threadworms.

VERRUCA

A verruca is a wart on the sole of the foot and it is caused by a highly contagious virus. Your child probably picked up the verruca at a swimming pool, or anywhere someone with a verruca has walked. A verruca can be especially painful because walking on it squashes it into the skin. Like warts verrucas often disappear of their own accord after a time, but because they are painful it may be advisable to seek treatment.

WHAT TO LOOK OUT FOR

- Small, round swelling on the sole of the foot, possibly brownish coloured
- Pain when walking or putting weight on the foot

HOW TO TREAT A VERRUCA

- Apply a proprietary wart ointment, plaster or liquid to the verruca. Repeat until the verruca disappears.
- If your child goes swimming cover the verruca with a waterproof plaster.
- If the verruca fails to respond to treatment or becomes particularly

troublesome, see the doctor or a chiropodist, who may treat it with a freezing agent or alternatively soften and scrape it until it disappears. The latter treatment may need several courses over a few weeks.

See also: Warts.

VOMITING

Vomiting is usually less distressing in a child than in an adult. Treatment depends very much on the nature of the vomiting and any accompanying symptoms. The main types are listed below.

WHAT TO LOOK OUT FOR

1. Vomiting in a baby, when she regurgitates a little milk during or after feeding.
   Cause: Such 'possetting', as it is called, is normal. As the baby burps she brings up a little of the feed with the wind. Try to avoid sudden changes of position, such as sitting your baby bolt upright after a feed. Lie her on her side so that any regurgitated milk drains away.
2. Vomiting in a baby under ten weeks that is sudden, projectile and forceful.
   Cause: Could be pyloric stenosis (see page 129).
3. Vomiting accompanied by a runny nose or a cough.
   Cause: Cold or cough (see page 69 and page 79).
4. Vomiting with general symptoms of unwellness, accompanied by diarrhoea.
   Cause: Possible food poisoning (see page 97) or gastroenteritis (see page 99). This could be serious in a young baby, so consult the doctor.
5. Vomiting accompanied by a red face and feeling of heat, plus any other symptoms such as cough, cold or earache.
   Cause: Infection of some sort. Urinary infections and ear infections are often accompanied by vomiting.
6. Vomiting when travelling in a car, boat or plane. The child becomes pale and listless and complains of feeling sick.
   Cause: Travel sickness (see page 157).
7. Vomiting accompanied by abdominal pain.
   Cause: Possible appendicitis (see page 54).

8. Vomiting with bowel motions that are red and lumpy. Spasms of
   severe pain.
   Cause: Intussusception (see page 116).
9. Vomiting accompanied by stiff neck and dislike of bright light.
   Cause: Meningitis.

HOW TO TREAT VOMITING

- In the case of vomiting that suggests gastroenteritis, appendicitis,
  intussusception or meningitis, consult the doctor straight away. See
  also the relevent entries in this book.
- For other, less serious vomiting let your child lie on a couch or bed
  and provide her with a container in which to vomit.
- Don't force your child to eat, but give her frequent sips of water or
  rehydrating mixture.
- Check your child's temperature to see whether she is running a
  fever, and treat accordingly (see page 96).
- The main danger of vomiting is dehydration, so if you suspect your
  child is becoming dehydrated consult the doctor. Your child may
  need to be admitted to hospital to treat or prevent dehydration.
- Once your child has stopped being sick, reintroduce solid foods
  gradually. Milk, and bland foods such as jelly, blancmange, fish or
  lightly cooked chicken, are most suitable.

See also: Abdominal pain; Allergies; Dehydration; Fever.

WARTS

A wart is a small, solid growth caused by a virus, which is spread by
direct contact with someone else with a wart. Like verrucas they often
disappear spontaneously after a few months or years.

Sometimes warts appear in crops, most commonly on the hands but
also on the face, neck, arms, legs, even genitals. When a wart appears
on the foot it is known as a verruca.

WHAT TO LOOK OUT FOR

- Small, horny swellings either alone or in crops
- Tiny, dark-red or blackish spots in the centre of the wart – these are
  blood vessels supplying the wart with nourishment

HOW TO TREAT WARTS

- Many warts disappear of their own accord. If not, or if the wart is unsightly or on a part of the body such as the hand where it could infect others, buy a proprietary wart preparation from the chemist. Read the instructions carefully to avoid putting it on healthy skin. Do not apply to the face or genitals.
- If the warts persist despite treatment, or if they are on your child's face or genitals, consult the doctor. He or she may freeze the wart off with dry ice or liquid nitrogen, burn it off with a strong acid or heated needle, or scrape it off over a period of weeks.
- Discourage your child from scratching warts as this will cause them to spread to other parts of the skin.

See also: Verruca.

WAX IN THE EARS

Wax is produced by the ear for lubrication and to protect it from dirt and infection. It works its way to the outside of ear, where it can be cleaned away using a piece of cotton wool. Excess wax can be associated with otitis media, and occasionally surplus wax can build up and affect the hearing.

WHAT TO LOOK OUT FOR

- Deafness – your child does not respond if you speak to her softly or when she cannot see you
- Complaints of noises or a feeling of fullness in the ear
- Visible build-up of wax in the ear

HOW TO TREAT WAX IN THE EARS

- Clean away any excess wax at the opening of the ear canal using a piece of cotton wool. Never poke anything in the ear such as a cotton bud, as you risk pushing the wax even further down and damaging the delicate ear drum.
- Consult the doctor, who will examine your child's ears and suggest a course of treatment. This may consist of putting warmed ear drops

(available from the chemist) into your child's ears for several nights to dissolve the wax. If the wax does not clear your child may need to have her ears syringed out.
- Some children are prone to a build-up of wax; if your child is, keep her ears clear by washing them out with soap once a week (beware of using cotton buds, you could damage the ear drum) and be alert for future build-ups which will need to be treated.

See also: Deafness; Otitis media.

Whooping cough

Whooping cough begins like an ordinary cold and cough but in fact is an extremely serious illness, especially for babies under six months. It has an incubation period of 7 to 21 days, then shortly afterwards the coughing starts to occur in spasms, making it difficult to take a breath in. The 'whoop' is the only way the child can draw breath, and is the noise created as air rushes past the swollen larynx. The coughing fit is usually followed by vomiting. Small babies cannot learn the knack of whooping to get air into their lungs, and every year several babies die of whooping cough. Most of these deaths could have been avoided if the babies had been vaccinated against the disease, although it can occur even before they are old enough to be immunized. In recent years there has been some controversy over the whooping cough vaccine. However, research shows that the dangers of the illness, which can have very serious complications, outweigh the risk of damage from the vaccine. Statistically, one authority has estimated that a health visitor would have had to have been working since Roman times before she would have seen one case of a child brain-damaged by the whooping cough vaccine. A very few babies might be vulnerable to the vaccine, for example those with existing brain problems. If you are in any doubt, discuss the matter with your doctor.

WHAT TO LOOK OUT FOR
- Common cold symptoms such as raised temperature, cough, mucus, aches and pains
- Spasms of coughing which end in a 'whoop'

- Vomiting after a coughing fit
- Inability to sleep

HOW TO TREAT WHOOPING COUGH

- If you suspect whooping cough, call the doctor. Keep your child away from other children and babies. If the disease is caught early enough, antibiotics may lessen the severity of the infection. However, your child may have already had the illness for some time before he sees the doctor, since the early symptoms are similar to those of an upper respiratory infection.
- Hold your child upright during a coughing fit. Raising the foot of your baby's bed may help drain phlegm.
- If your child is sick after a coughing fit, offer him a small snack and a drink, or a feed if he is breast- or bottle-fed. He is more likely to keep it down at this stage.
- In severe cases your child may need to be admitted to hospital so that he has back-up facilities should he become dehydrated or have problems breathing.
- If your child develops breathing difficulties after seeming to get better, he might have contracted a secondary lung infection such as bronchitis or pneumonia. Contact the doctor.
- Don't worry if next time your child gets a cough he starts to 'whoop' – it is not because he has caught whooping cough again but simply because he has learnt the trick of whooping.

See also: Bronchitis; Dehydration; Pneumonia.